Woking

A Chronology of the

19th and 20th Centuries

Jim Bell

First Published 2021

Copyright © Jim Bell

All rights reserved

Published by

The Wokingham Society

chairman@wokinghamsociety.org.uk

ISBN 978-1-871514-04-9

Every effort has been made to establish copyright and permission has been obtained to reproduce pictures where required, but if any copyright images have been used inadvertently sincere apologies are tendered.

Illustrations
Unless otherwise stated the photographs are from the Ken Goatley collection.

Front cover illustration
drawing of the Town Hall by Ken Head, courtesy of The Wokingham Society

Back cover illustrations
upper   Painting by Pitman from a photograph of Broad Street in the 1860s, courtesy of Wokingham Town Council

middle Boer War celebration 1903
lower   Youth and Community Centre by Jim Bell

Contents

Preface	i
The Chronology	1
Addendum	213
Sources	214
Other Publications by Jim Bell	215

In memory of my good friends Ken and Edna Goatley.

Preface

In 1977 the History Group of the Wokingham Society produced *Wokingham: A Chronology*, which recorded events from the town's history from the Middle Ages to the mid-20th Century. Its fourth edition took the story up to 1986 but the book has long been out of print.

My first thought was to update the book but I came to the conclusion that it might be better to produce a larger work (the Chronology was 50 pages long) which covered a shorter period but, being based on my extensive collection of newspaper articles from the local press, could paint a more varied picture of Wokingham from the beginning of the 19th Century to the end of the last one.

This has meant that local events can, where appropriate, be put into a wider national or international context, but also that the ephemeral and sometimes whimsical aspects can rub shoulders with the more sober and important developments in the town's life. In addition, greater length has also allowed particular brief reports in the earlier *Chronology* to be fleshed out in greater detail.

The coincidence of the starting point in the early 1800s with the development of photography has allowed the use of pictures to illustrate the items included so that we can not only read about individual lives and activities but see them as they were at the time.

In the process of compiling this book I have been grateful to receive information and advice from colleagues but particular thanks are due to Peter Must, Chairman of the Wokingham Society, who proof-read the text as it emerged and made many suggestions for clarification or amendment; and to Paul King, editor of *Late Victorian Wokingham* and author of *Wokingham Market Place 1900 – 2019*, who shaped the work into its final form and prepared it for publication.

Lastly, many thanks to the Executive Committee of the Wokingham Society for providing a grant which has enabled this book to be published.

Jim Bell

Steamer fire engine delivered to Wokingham Fire Brigade on April 21st 1891 and christened Alert by Mrs. Murdoch, wife of MP for Reading. The horses are Tilling Greys donated by the 6th Marquis of Downshire.

1802 - 1810

1802

March 31st

The people of Wokingham celebrated the signing of the Treaty of Amiens, ending the initial period of hostilities between France and a number of European monarchies which commenced in 1792. Prominent in the celebrations was the Wokingham Volunteer Association (also known as the Forest Volunteers), established by Royal commission at the outbreak of war, with James Webb as its Captain Commandant.

May 4th

Peace was officially proclaimed at Wokingham after which James Webb, Commander of the Volunteer Association, read the thanks of Parliament to his men. The corps was then disbanded.

July 28th

An elegant three quart gilt tankard and cover were presented to James Webb as a token of gratitude from the people of Wokingham.

1803

August

Following the commencement of the Napoleonic Wars the Wokingham Volunteers, comprising two companies each of 70 men, were re-established under Captain James Webb.

1808

The Local Militia was created and the Volunteers were disbanded.

June 12th

A Baptist Sunday School was started at the meeting house in Milton Road, then Nonsuch Lane, with twenty boys and twenty girls.

1809

October 24/25th

The people of Wokingham celebrated the Golden Jubilee of King George III with a ball in the Town Hall on the 24th. The following day was greeted by the bells from the church tower and three volleys of musketry from the Market Place.

1810 - 1817

1810

The Baptist church building was enlarged and modified by adding a new vestry and lengthening the building by sixteen and a half feet.

1812

November 16th

John Walter I died. He was an English newspaper publisher and founder of *The Times* newspaper, which he launched in January 1785 as *The Daily Universal Register*. He also played a leading part in establishing the Coal Exchange in London. He was born in London and was educated at Merchant Taylors' School, then located in London.

John Walter I

1813

The Windsor Forest Enclosure Act was passed. This enabled the Crown to retain 6,500 acres of the old forest with 1,500 acres of mature woodland in the Cranbourne area where many earlier Keepers of the Forest had made their home. About 3,000 acres were set aside for deer and cattle and could not be cultivated.

1816

October

John Walter II, son of the founder of *The Times* newspaper, purchased 158 acres of Bearwood and 146 adjoining acres from the Crown, at a cost of £3, 050 for the land and £7, 964 for the timber.

1817

A Wesleyan Society was established in Wokingham. The location of the meetings was unclear.

1818 - 1824

March 27th

A duel was fought in the Cock Pit by two young men who were unaware that their pistols had been loaded with gunpowder but no bullets.

June 18th

A division of the Royal Horse Guards stationed in Wokingham celebrated the anniversary of the Battle of Waterloo with a public dinner.

October 4th

A pot containing a thousand Roman copper coins was found by workmen in a field near Wokingham.

1818

Stephen Sale (1799-1881) established his seed business which was to be the basis of Sale and Sons, Wokingham. In the same year he went on foot to the company of Hugh Ronald and Son of Brentford, London, who supplied his initial stock. It was delivered in May at a cost of £16 13s 3d.

November 19th

The Wokingham Savings Bank was established.

1819

A site in Rose Street was purchased in the name of the Rev. John Waterhouse. Arrangements were made for a barn which stood on the site to be made into a chapel.

1820

The Wesleyan Barn Chapel was opened in Rose Street.

1821

Bull baiting was prohibited by the Corporation for humanitarian reasons. George Staverton (d. 1661) had left a will that provided two bulls each year to be tethered in the Market Place to be baited by dogs. For betting purposes, bulldogs would be set upon the beast one after another, to try to fasten their teeth in the cartilage of the bull's nose. When a dog succeeded he was acclaimed for a 'pin'.

1824 - 1826

1824

March 15th

Caroline Bird (1805-1841), daughter of Charles Bird of Matthews Green House, was converted to Methodism. She carried out much religious work in the poverty stricken homes in the over-crowded courts off Rose Street.

1825

A National School was erected in Rose Street for 250 boys and girls.

Wokingham's first cricket club was founded.

February 28th

The 9th High Steward of Wokingham, Richard Aldworth Griffin-Neville 2nd Baron Braybrooke, died and the position of 10th High Steward devolved to his eldest son Richard Griffin-Neville 3rd Baron Braybrooke.

Richard Aldworth Griffin-Neville
2nd Baron Braybrooke (1750-1825)

Richard Griffin-Neville
3rd Baron Braybrooke (1783-1858)

April 6th

Paul Houlton was elected Alderman and Chief Magistrate of Wokingham.

1826

A Baptist school consisting of eight boys and eight girls was opened under the control of Mr. and Mrs James Sale, Jnr. Only Baptist children were allowed to attend.

1827 - 1833

1827
The Baptist church was again enlarged.

1828
The Test and Corporation Acts were repealed. The removal of disabilities under these Acts meant that Nonconformists could hold municipal office; William Heelas Snr. (1776-1856) proprietor of Heelas and Sons, Market Place and farmer, was soon after elected Alderman.

1830

January 1st

The Wokingham Theatre production of *Speed the Plough*, a comedy by Thomas Morton, was a great success.

November 19th

At a meeting held in Wokingham Guild Hall it was decided to form branches of special constables to fight fires and apprehend arsonists.

1831
The last silk mill in Wokingham was closed.

1833
Last bull baiting in England. An Act of Parliament consolidated an Act of 1827 which banned the cruel and inhumane treatment of cattle by including bull baiting. Bulls were still provided at Christmas and the meat distributed to the poor.

June 11th

The first meeting of the East Berks Archery Club was held at Luckley House.

December 18th

A meeting was held in the Parish Church to discuss the best way of employing the poor during winter.

1835 - 1837

All Saints Parish Church

1835

The Wokingham Agricultural Association was founded.

August 1st

Wokingham Poor Law Union was formed. Its operation was overseen by an elected Board of Guardians numbering 20 representing 16 constituent parishes.

September 9th

Caroline Bird married William Heelas, Jnr. (1801-1864), who was a pillar of the Baptists, at All Saints Church.

1836

Wokingham ceased to be part of Salisbury Diocese when the parish of Wokingham, with the rest of the Archdeaconry of Berkshire, was transferred to the Diocese of Oxford.

The Baptist School was made available to children of any denomination.

1837

The old Manor House of Evendons was demolished and the building of a second house commenced.

June 20th

King William IV died at Windsor Castle and Princess Alexandrina Victoria became Queen.

1838 - 1843

1838

June 28th

Princess Alexandrina Victoria was crowned Queen of the United Kingdom of Great Britain and Ireland.

1840

The Paddington to Reading railway line was opened.

The Tablet, a weekly publication for the Catholic community in England, was founded by Frederick Lucas, a distinguished Wokingham inhabitant. Born and educated as a Quaker, he was converted to Catholicism in 1839 and later became M.P. for Meath.

1841

July 26th

The British School in Milton Road, then Nonsuch Lane, was opened for some 230 children.

1842

Palmer Girls' School (Maiden School) was amalgamated with the National School.

The building occupied by Charles Palmer Boys' School, already amalgamated with the National School, in Down (later Denmark) Street was later demolished and the materials used to construct the Infants' School behind 33 Rose Street.

The Primitive Methodists came to Wokingham.

July 20th

A lodge of the Independent Order of Odd Fellows, Manchester Unit, to be called the "Royal Forest Lodge," was founded at the King's Head Inn.

November 3rd

A fire severely damaged Bearwood House.

1843

Charles Kingsley, author of *The Water Babies* etc., became Rector of Eversley.

1844 - 1845

The Primitive Methodists, *Ranters*, rented a room in Wokingham.

The disused Charles Palmer Boys' School was demolished and the materials were used to construct the Infants' School on the premises of the Martha Palmer Charity in Rose Street.

1844

October

John Wise, the landlord of the Rose Inn, moved the inn to its present site and converted it into a commercial inn with lock-up coach-houses and stabling.

The Old Rose Inn

1845

The whole of Wokingham came into Berkshire.

Thomas A. Readwin published his book, *An Account of the Charities of the town and Parish of Wokingham.*

Concern was expressed by the churchwardens about the dilapidated condition of All Saints' Parish Church.

January 20th

Queen Victoria and Prince Albert passed through Wokingham to visit the Duke of Wellington at Stratfield Saye. Alderman Thomas Creaker presented her Majesty with a scroll In the Market Place.

1846 - 1846

Queen Victoria and Prince Albert pass through Wokingham
London Illustrated

1846

April 23rd

St. Catherine's Church, Bearwood, was consecrated by the Bishop of Salisbury, Samuel Wilberforce. The church was built by John Walter II and named in memory of his daughter, Catherine Mary, who died of a chill in 1844.

St. Catherine's Parish Church, Bearwood

Ecclesiastical peculiars, including that of the Dean of Salisbury's Peculiar of Wokingham, were abolished. The patronage of All Saints was transferred from the Dean to the Diocese of the Bishop of Oxford.

1847 - 1848

A report found that conditions in the Wokingham Workhouse in Down Street (Denmark Street) were too cramped. Rooms were damp and badly ventilated and there were no infirmary and fever wards.

May

Bearwood became a parish. The boundaries stretched eastwards from Loddon Bridge to Emmbrook and southwards to Arborfield Cross and contained parts of the old parishes of Hurst and Wokingham. They also included the Liberty of Newland and Sindlesham.

1847

The Wokingham Gas Company opened on a site off Finchampstead Road.

July 28th

John Walter II of Bearwood died.

John Walter II (1776-1847)

1848

It was planned to build a new workhouse for 250 inmates at a site on the northern side of Barkham Road on land purchased from Mr. George Howell. A competition was held to design the new workhouse and the prize of £50 was won by Mr. Richard Billing of Reading. The contract to build at a cost of £6,200 went to Mr Trugo of London.

1849 - 1850

1849

January

Work to build the new workhouse in Barkham Road commenced.

July 4th

The railway line from Reading to Guildford and then to Dorking and Redhill was opened. The railway was built by an independent company under the *Staines, Wokingham and Woking Junction Railway Act.*. The first train on the new line from Reading to Guildford via Wokingham arrived in Wokingham at 8 am.

Wokingham Railway Station

1850

The Public Libraries Act of 1850 enabled town councils to establish public libraries and museums. The act, however, was unsatisfactory because it placed many limitations on the type of council that could adopt it, the amount of money that the boroughs were permitted to spend and the ways in which this money could be spent.

A room in Down Street (Denmark Street) was registered in the name of the Primitive Methodists.

1852 - 1855

August 6th

The new workhouse, now Wokingham Hospital, in Barkham Road, was opened.

The new workhouse © Peter Higginbotham

1852

The Garth Hunt was founded by Thomas Colleton Garth.

1854

March

The Great Western Coal Company opened a depot in Broad Street.

September

A cholera epidemic broke out in Wokingham.

1855

The Public Library Acts of 1855 and 1866 eliminated the population limits, allowing even very small towns or parishes to set up a public library.

July 3rd

The Corn Market was formally re-opened.

September 11th

Wokingham celebrated the fall of Sevastopol. The siege of Sevastopol

1856 - 1858

lasted from October 1854 until September 1855 during the Crimean War. The allies comprising French, Sardinia, Ottoman, and British forces landed at Eupatoria in September 1854 with 50,000 men intending to make a triumphal march to Sebastopol, the capital of the Crimea, After a year of fighting against the Russians who occupied the city the Russian army withdrew before the allies could encircle it.

1856

June 2nd

It was decided to postpone the official holiday to celebrate the end of the Crimean War to June 2nd to enable the maximum number of people to enjoy this event together with the laying of the foundation stone of Wellington College by Queen Victoria.

July 9th

The London and South Western Railway Company opened a line from Staines to Wokingham via Ascot.

1857

July 30th

Private Robert Lockart of the Royal Scots Greys died on a route march from Farnham to Wokingham.

1858

March 13th

The 10th High Steward of Wokingham, Richard Griffin-Neville, 3rd Baron Braybrooke died and the position of 11th High Steward devolved to his son, Richard Cornwallis Neville, 4th Baron Braybrooke.

May

It was resolved at a meeting to replace Wokingham Guild Hall with a new Town Hall.

July

The proposed design of the new Town Hall by Messrs. Poulton and Woodman was accepted.

1860 - 1860

September 2nd

It was resolved unanimously to accept the tender of Mr. Woodroffe, builder, of Reading to build the new Town Hall.

September 13th

A farewell ball was held in the Old Guild Hall.

The old Guild Hall was demolished.

1860

The present Easthampstead Park was rebuilt.

The old almshouses in Down Street (later Denmark Street) were demolished.

Isaiah Gadd, an 18 year old draper's assistant from Gloucestershire, came to work at Heelas' in Wokingham.

All Saints' Parish Church was closed for intended restoration.

February

Sir Edward Walter (1824-1904) founded the Corps of Commissionaires as a way to provide gainful employment for ex-servicemen on return from the Crimean War.

March

The preliminary steps for the formation of Wokingham Rifle Corps were taken. Thirty volunteers entered their names.

June 6th

The new Town Hall was opened by the High Steward of Wokingham, Richard Cornwallis Neville, 4th Lord Braybrooke.

June 18th

The Savings Bank weekly meeting was held for the first time in the room in the new Town Hall. The room, which was in the corner of the new building facing the Rose Hotel, was large and suited for the bank purposes. The bank was to open every Monday as usual from 12.00 till one o'clock.

1860 - 1860

June

The Police Fire Brigade moved into the Town Hall.

Wokingham Town Hall by Ken Head

July

Work to build the Baptist Church in Milton Road commenced.

August 4th

The foundation stone of the new Baptist Church was laid by the Rev. John Hinton M.A.

August

The members of the Literary Institute took possession of the room in the north end of the Town Hall on the ground floor facing Broad Street, which was granted to them by the Corporation.

1861 - 1862

1861

February 6th

It was decided to proceed with the restoration of All Saints' Parish Church. Commander Elliott Morres R.N. gave a bond of £5,000 should it be required.

February 21st

The 11th High Steward of Wokingham, Richard Cornwallis Neville, 4th Lord Braybrooke, died and the position of 12th High Steward devolved to his brother, Charles Cornwallis Neville, 5th Baron Braybrooke (1823-1902).

April 3rd

A meeting of the 6th Berks Volunteers to elect officers was held in Wokingham Town Hall.

July 28th

The first service was held in the new Baptist Chapel in Milton Road.

The Baptist Chapel, Wokingham by Ken Head

1862

July

A sufficient sum of money had been collected to enable the restoration of All Saints' Parish Church to commence.

1863 - 1864

September 2nd

Mrs. John Walter III laid the foundation stone of St. Paul's Parish Church, Wokingham.

1863

Charles Kingsley's book "The Water Babies" was published. The boy sweep, Tom, who came down in the wrong bedroom, was said to be based on Sooty Seaward, a Chimney sweep of Wokingham who became an alderman.

March 10th

The people of Wokingham celebrated the wedding of the Prince of Wales and Princess Alexandra of Denmark. The name of Down Street was changed to Denmark Street to commemorate the wedding.

July 27th

St. Paul's Parish, Wokingham, was founded, by Order of Her Majesty in Council, The new parish comprised part of the ancient Parish of Wokingham and a small portion of the Parish of St. Catherine of Bearwood totalling approximately 2,200 acres.

1864

April 15th

All Saints' Parish Church was opened after renovations.

St. Paul's Parish Church, Wokingham

July 23rd

St. Paul's Parish Church was consecrated by Bishop Samuel Wilberforce, Bishop of Oxford.

1865 - 1866

October

The larger fire engine that was kept at Wokingham Town Hall underwent extensive alterations and repairs. For this purpose Mr. Merryweather of the firm of Merryweather and Sons, suggested what repairs and alterations were necessary. Mr. Alderman Ferguson ordered that these should be carried out at once.

December 22nd

The Working Men's Club was established.

1865

Work commenced to build a larger Bearwood mansion.

February 6th

The Working Men's Club was very popular and the rooms were filled every night by the members who had joined in large numbers and who appreciated the comforts and social recreation provided. The opening of the Club was celebrated by a social soiree for the members and their wives and friends.

June

The first issue of *The Wokingham Parish Magazine* appeared. It was published every month and at first contained news from St. Paul's and All Saints' Parish Churches plus local information. St. Sebastian's Parish Church later contributed as well.

June

The first intimation of Wokingham having a lending library appeared in the first issue of the *Wokingham Parish Magazine.* " *Attendance is given to the Lending Library every alternate Saturday, in the Bank Room, from eleven o'clock till one o'clock.*"

1866

A second cholera epidemic broke out in Wokingham.

January

A book depot was created at Emmbrook. Larger subscriptions were requested to enable the Lending Library to provide books to both parishes.

1867 - 1868

June

The Vestry Committee appointed Police Supt. Millard as inspector of nuisances for the south district of the Wokingham Union, and Mr. Herrington of Twyford inspector of the north district. They were to be responsible for complaints relating to the sanitation, sewage disposal and water supply.

October 15th

St. Paul's Parish Schools at Shute End, built by John Walter III, were opened. The architect was Henry Woodyer and the first headmaster was Mr. George Jameson.

November 12th

It was proposed to open a new branch of the Parish Lending Library at Mrs. Brant's on the Forest Road where books would be lent on the second Monday of the month at eleven o'clock.

1867

The position of Beadle was discontinued.

Work commenced to build a rectory for St. Paul's Church.

February

The cost of the new clock and bells recently erected in the Town Hall was defrayed by public subscription collected under the supervision of Alderman Skerritt. The clock showed the time on four dials and struck the quarters and hours on bells which weighed about 4 hundredweights and had been cast by Steinbank & Mears of Whitechapel.

1868

November 1st

At mid-day the Windsor Forest Turnpike Trust expired after an existence of about a century.

1869 - 1870

7th December

A gale blew down the remaining elm tree in the Market Place on which, for many years, spectators at bull-baiting had taken refuge.

The elm tree

1869

November

The trustees of the Wesleyan Church purchased the *Eagle Brewery* that stood behind their chapel to enable a larger chapel to be built.

1870

January

Because of the intended opening of the Electric Telegraph at the Post Office it was found that the accommodation at the former office was too restricted. Mr. Spencer, the Postmaster, therefore fitted up the house adjoining the former office for the combined offices for the Telegraph and Post.

May 11th

The foundation stone of the new Wesleyan Chapel was laid by Sir Frances Lycett, a British businessman and philanthropist, and a prominent member of the Methodist Church. .

1870 - 1870

July 20th

St. Paul's Parish Church Rectory was consecrated by the Bishop of Oxford.

St. Paul's Parish Church Rectory

November 10th

The new Wesleyan Chapel in Rose Street was opened when the Rev. Samuel Coley conducted the first service. It occupied the sites of the old Barn Methodist Chapel and of the Eagle Brewery that stood behind it.

The new Wesleyan Chapel

1871 - 1871

December 24th

John Balston Walter, the eldest son of John Walter III, died in the evening of Christmas Eve while skating on one of the lakes of the Bearwood Estate with some relatives. The ice gave way and two of his brothers and a cousin fell into the water and were in danger of drowning. John went to the rescue, but almost immediately the sudden shock of the icy water stopped his heart.

1871

Keep Hatch House was built by the Rev. George E. Denis de Vitré after his return from India.

Keep Hatch House

February

The Wesleyan trustees purchased land off Rose Street to accommodate Sunday school buildings. The land comprised the plot immediately behind the brew house site together with the cottage adjoining the passage at the side of the chapel.

April

The monthly *Wokingham Methodist Messenger* was launched at a price of 1d.

July

Wokingham's first brass band, comprising players from St. Paul's and All Saints' Parish Churches, was formed.

1872 - 1872

July

A meeting was held in Wokingham Town Hall to discuss the concern of the people about the inadequate sanitation, sewage disposal and water supply. Although a considerable amount of money had been spent on solving problems there was little to show for it. A proposal was made to replace the Vestry Committee with a more efficient authority. The meeting was adjourned.

November

Provision was made to form a Reading Room at St. Paul's Schools for the young men of the town.

November 2nd and 3rd

The annual November pleasure fair was held and the weather was fine. There were numerous stalls, shows, shooting galleries and roundabouts. The roundabouts, two driven by steam, especially seemed to be popular. Superintendent Millard and several constables kept such a vigil eye that there was no robbery or disturbance.

1872

January 30th

At the meeting to discuss the problems of sanitation Mr. Soames, solicitor, appeared for the people but there was no one to represent the Vestry Committee. Mr. Frankum, solicitor, representing those who had not complained, requested that a reply from the Vestry Committee be considered. It appeared that this Special Drainage District Wahad been formed in 1866, and that the Vestry had appointed a committee for one year. The committee had met once, but there was no record for that meeting, and little had been done by the Sewer Authority up to the present time. Mr. Soames, who was a member of the committee, apologised for this inactivity by saying that there was a complication of authorities in the town which paralysed the action of the Vestry Committee.

February

Work commenced to enlarge St. Paul's Parish Church.

1873 - 1873

February 21st

The inspector from the Local Government Board revealed that the drinking water supplied to the residents of Wokingham was unfit for human consumption and the facilities for the disposal of sewage were inadequate. All but one of the wells were closed.

February 29th

A letter was sent to the Vestry Committee, as the Sewer authority of Wokingham, by the Local Government Board, Whitehall. Attached was a copy of the results of Inspector John Harrison's survey of Wokingham which found the sanitation of Wokingham to be inadequate, the quality of the water from the wells below Wokingham to be 'unquestionably abominable', and the number of toilets available to the public to be insufficient. Mr. Harrison ordered most of the wells to be closed immediately and recommended that remedial action be taken as soon as possible.

May

The new Wesleyan Sunday School in Rose Street was opened.

July 1st

Thomas Wescott's timber yard and saw mills in Peach Street were entirely destroyed by fire.

1873

April 28th

A meeting chaired by the inspector from the Local Government Board heard evidence relating to a petition received from the townspeople requesting the formation of a district, comprising the town and its suburb to be called "The District of Wokingham," under the Local Government Act.

July 14th

The first Parish Room of St. Paul's Church at the Terrace was opened.

July 28th

The foundation stone of the north aisle of St. Paul's Parish Church was laid by Mrs. Brown, wife of the Rector, the Rev. Joseph Brown.

1874 - 1874

September 19th

The foundation stone of All Saints' Rectory was laid.

1874

Bearwood mansion was completed. It was said to have rivalled Windsor Castle in size and opulence which was perhaps why Queen Victoria was thought to have disliked John Walter III.

Bearwood Mansion courtesy Arborfield Local History Society

January

St. Paul's Church was reopened after enlargement and restoration.

April

From this month onwards of all the lending libraries only the one in Wokingham Town Hall was mentioned in Parish Magazine notices.

June 2nd

The Wokingham Fair was abolished by the Home Secretary at the request of the people of Wokingham.

1875 - 1876

June

A Board was formed under the Local Government Board to administer the Public Health Acts.

September 24th

The foundation stone of All Saints Schools (Palmer Schools) in Rectory Road was laid by Mrs. John Walter III.

1875

Wokingham Town Football Club was founded.

January 1st

The Act to regulate the employment of children in agriculture came into force.

September 30th

The benediction of the recently completed Palmer Schools was performed, by the Bishop of Oxford, Dr. Mackarness.

1876

Heelas of Wokingham opened a savings bank for customers.

May 13th

In accordance with the Explosives Act 1875 the Justice in Petty Sessions appointed Supt. Millard Inspector of Premises for the Wokingham Division, dealing with locations where fireworks or other explosives were made or kept.

September 29th

It was resolved to form a volunteer fire brigade for Wokingham and the surrounding neighbourhood.

The earliest known photograph of the Wokingham Volunteer Fire Brigade

1877 - 1878

October

The commissioners appointed to inquire into the existing condition of unreformed corporations publicly requested that anyone having any information about the Corporation of Wokingham should write to them at Westminster.

November 14th

The commission appointed to inquire into the existing condition of unreformed corporations questioned the town clerk of Wokingham at a meeting in Whitehall as to the powers, duties, and responsibilities of the Corporation and its officials. They also examined the town's charters, sessional records, minutes, and accounts.

November 14th

The first of the entertainments which were usually held during the winter took place at the Town Hall. Charles T. Murdoch of Buckhurst was in the chair. These entertainments had been held for the previous few years and had been found useful in providing amusement for the townspeople. The profits were divided between the Working Men's and the British Workmen Clubs,

1877

May

While a decayed post, which for many years had formed part of an old out-house on the premises of Mrs. Ludlow, Rose Street, was being broken up, eighteen gold coins of the reign of Richard II, were discovered in an excellent state of preservation. They had been carefully wrapped in coarse canvas and concealed in a deep mortise.

1878

March 21st

The Wokingham Voluntary Fire Brigade met in the grounds of St. Paul's Rectory by permission of the Rev. Joseph T. Brown, to test their new manual fire engine recently ordered from Messrs. Merryweather. The engine and some hose, ladders etc cost £170. The engine was very powerful, being capable of shooting 136 gallons of water a minute to a height of 130 feet. It was fitted with a pair of 7-inch pumps, operated by

1879 - 1879

thirty men. The tests, witnessed by a number of people, were highly satisfactory.

May 28th

A meeting was held at the Town Hall to consider the proposed scheme of the Wokingham District Water (Company) Limited to supply pure water to the town. Alderman. J. L. Roberts presided, The proposal was approved.

October

The despatch of letters at 1.30pm was abolished and instead a letter bag was filled at 3pm for London and all parts except Reading. Letters for Sandhurst and Wellington College had to be posted before 9.30 pm.

December 24th

On Christmas Eve the Amateur Band went around the town playing well-known Christmas hymns and carols. Ordinarily bands followed up their performances by ringing bells and asking for money but the members of the Wokingham Band gave their services free in order to usher in the festival amongst the townspeople in a suitable manner. They were led by Mr. Breacher who set the tunes expressly for the various instruments.

1879

January 23rd

Mr. Goodchild, the ex-Alderman, invited his fellow townspeople to spend an evening on the ice on the ornamental water on his property at Waterloo Lodge. The large space was lit by burning tar barrels, Chinese lanterns and torches. Between 300 and 400 people assembled and all appeared to enjoy themselves. Messrs. L and T Carroll, Messrs. H and H Roberts and others formed themselves into a glee party and sang some part-songs and glees.

The handbell ringers were also present to entertain the crowd. A large fire was kept burning on the central island where a fireworks display took place. Mr. William Chambers supplied the refreshments.

February

The annual report of Dr. Shea, the Medical Officer of Health was presented to the Local Board. In 1878 there were 98 births and 60 deaths

1880 - 1880

in the district. Of the births 48 were males, and 50 females; of the deaths, 29 were males, and 31 females. Out of the 60 deaths, 17 took place in the Union Workhouse, and of those 12 belonged to the rural district, leaving 58 to be credited to the town, giving a death-rate of 18.7 per 1,000. This was an increase on the rate for 1877, which was abnormally low. The year 1878 was, however, characterised by a high death-rate throughout the country. The report contained details of ages and the various causes of death. A statement was also shown of the work done by the Inspector of Nuisances, from which it was seen that 110 cases of nuisance had been remedied, and that much had been accomplished in improving the sanitary states of locations which had for a long time been considered sources of danger to health. The report noticed the improvements effected in paving and channelling during the past year, and ended by congratulating the town on the favourable return as to its exceptional freedom from acute infectious disease

April 21st

The Royal District Bicycle Club held its opening run on Easter Monday.

1880

April 21st

Wokingham Water Company found an abundant supply of pure water 340 feet below ground near Finchampstead Road, between the brook and South Eastern railway. It was estimated to yield about 360,000 gallons a day.

May 11th

The Board of Management of Berkshire Hospital agreed to supply a trained nurse to visit the working class sick in their own homes.

June 1st

The Timber and Flour Mills of Peach Street, Wokingham, owned by Thomas Manley Wescott, were put up for sale by auction at The Mart, Tokenhouse Yard, London, by Weeks & Watts, Auctioneers.

June 2nd

The Guildford and Wokingham Cricket Clubs met for their first contest on Wokingham's ground. The match ended in a victory for the

1881 - 1881

Wokingham club by 14 runs. For Wokingham H. Baldwin was the only batsman to reach double figures, making 18 runs. None of the Guildford players scored double figures. R. Baldwin and Gater shared the bowling for Wokingham in the first innings of the visitors.. Baldwin bowled eight overs for 19 runs, while Gater bowled eight overs for eight runs, taking three wickets.

October

The Post Office Penny Savings Bank commenced.

October 20th

A meeting was held at the Town Hall for the purpose of establishing a musical Society for Wokingham. Mr. Murdoch proposed, and the Rev. Joseph T. Brown seconded "That a Musical Society be established in Wokingham during the winter months." The resolution was carried unanimously.

November 2nd

The first meeting of the Wokingham Musical Society was held in the Town Hall.

December

The tower of All Saints' Parish Church was restored.

1881

The Working Men's Club and the Working Men's Institute were amalgamated.

April 19th

John Walter III formally opened the Wokingham Water Works.

June

A new drinking fountain of polished Peterhead granite, a gift of the Rev. George E. Denis De Vitré, was erected outside Wokingham Town Hall opposite the Bush Hotel.

The drinking fountain

1882 - 1883

1882

The inhabitants of Wokingham petitioned the Privy Council for the grant of a Charter of Incorporation under the 1882 Act.

January 5th

The new rooms of the Wokingham Working Men's Club were opened by the Rector of All Saints' Church. The rooms were built behind the Coffee Tavern in Peach Street, which had opened in December. The rooms comprised a room for games, a reading room, and a third room for dressing, while the Coffee Tavern adjacent supplied refreshments in its own rooms. There were beds for those who needed lodgings overnight.

January 25th

The Drill Hall in Denmark Street was opened by Col. Sir R. Loyd Lindsay, V.C., M.P., at a dinner given by Captain Arthur Fraser Walter, eldest son of John Walter III who built the hall.

The Drill Hall

October

The Royal Berks Hospital provided Wokingham with its first ambulance carriage.

1883

The Unreformed Boroughs Act was passed. Unreformed boroughs were those corporate towns in England and Wales which had not been reformed

1884 - 1885

by the Municipal Corporations Act 1835, and the new Act finally forced the reform or dissolution of these corporations by 1886.

November

The South-Western Railway Company erected a wooden footbridge at Langborough Crossing.

1884

The Corporation of Wokingham was dissolved by an act of Parliament.

January 4th

A petition was addressed to her Majesty's Government by certain Wokingham householders who were hoping that a charter would be granted to the district whereby the powers and provisions of the Municipal Corporations Act would be extended.

October

Nurse Swadling, the Parish of Wokingham's first nurse, was appointed.

1885

Ownership of Holt House and Holt Estate land to the south side of Holt Lane passed from the Crutchley family to the Heelas family, owners of the Heelas drapers store in the Market Place.

July

The new Charter of Incorporation creating the Borough of Wokingham was issued by the Privy Council Office, and received in the town. By its provisions 12 Councillors were to be elected on Monday 2nd November and on 9th November the first Mayor was to be chosen. By the scheme of the Charter the boundary of the new Borough was the same as the limits of the existing Local Board, whose functions and duties would merge into the new Corporation in November, although it was believed that the Board would actually continue in existence until the following 25'th of March. It was hoped that the new status attained by the town would help to increase its importance and prosperity, and that the enlarged powers and duties conferred would be efficiently carried out for the benefit of the Borough of Wokingham, which was one of the oldest chartered Corporations in the country.

1885 - 1885

September 5th

Wokingham Chrysanthemum Society was founded to encourage the cultivation of the plant.

October 5th

The following is a contemporary summary of the Charter that was read out during the Council meeting:-

The Charter, for which a petition was presented in December 1883, is granted under the Municipal Corporations Act, 1882.

So much of the Parish of Wokingham as is within the limits of the existing Local Government District of Wokingham is created a Municipal Borough, by the name of the "Borough of Wokingham," the inhabitants to be one body politic and corporate by the name of the "Mayor, Aldermen, and Burgesses of the Borough of Wokingham, who may assume armorial bearings, and take and hold lands vested in them, or occupy lands or buildings necessary for their use, and shall have the powers and privileges usually invested by law in the Mayor, Aldermen, and Burgesses of Municipal Borough."

The number of Alderman to be four, and the number of Councillors to be twelve.

Henry Trower Roberts, solicitor, of Wokingham, or, in case of his death, refusal, or inability, John Frederick Sergeant, is to perform the duty of Town Clerk, and William Goodchild, of Wokingham, or, in default of him, Jas. Weeks is to perform the duties of mayor until the first election.

The first election is to take place on the 2nd of November next (Nov. 1st being Sunday), and the first meeting of the Council is to be held on the 9th of November.

The first schedule defines the boundary of the Borough, which is the same as the area under the jurisdiction of the Local Board.

The second schedule states that one-third of the Councillors, the four who are elected by the smallest number of votes, shall go out of office on Nov. 1st, 1886, another third, the four who received the next-smallest

1885 - 1885

number of votes, on Nov. 1st 1887, and the remaining third on Nov. 1st 1888. The two Aldermen who shall be elected by the smallest number votes to go out of office on Nov. 9th 1888, and the remaining two on Nov. 9th 1891.

October 26th

Mr. W. Goodchild, acting as Mayor for the Borough of Wokingham for the purpose of the first election of Town Councillors, sat in the Town Hall to hear objections against the nominations of some candidates. There were 29 nominations for the 12 seats, but some were nominated twice and some nomination papers were thrown out because of slight irregularities in completing the applications. Finally the number of candidates nominated was reduced to 21. Their names and descriptions being as follows:

C. Brant, butcher; H. Butler, grocer; G. Evans, saddler; W. Goodchild, gentleman; W. J. Goatlee, stationer; H. E. Hall, stationer; T. W. Heelas, draper; D. N. Heron, wine merchant; E. Ifould, butcher; F. Johnson, accountant; S. Knight, plumber; T. P. Major, gentleman; T. B. Martin, gentleman; W. Moorcock, gentleman; W. B. Mower, corn dealer; G.T. Phillips, timber merchant; G. Pigg, baker; G. Sale, furniture dealer; J. Watts, auctioneer; J. Wicks, gentleman; and T. M. Wescott, gentleman.

Polling was to take place on Monday.

November 7th

A special meeting of the old Corporation was held for the purpose of balancing the accounts to be handed over to the new Corporation on the following Monday. The Town Clerk, Mr. Frankum, produced the accounts which showed the sum of £600 invested in consols, £100 6s. 6d.at the bankers', and 9s. 1d. in the hands of the Town Clerk, which sums, after paying the cost of obtaining the new Charter became vested in the new Corporation on the 9th inst. They were accordingly ordered to be paid over to the new Borough Treasurer when appointed. A resolution was proposed and unanimously agreed upon that the members of the old Corporation on their dissolution begged to record their high opinion of the valuable and efficient services of their Town Clerk, Mr. Edward Frankum, in all matters relating to the office, and the accurate and satisfactory manner in which he had kept the accounts relating to Corporation property, for which they tendered him their best thanks.

1885 - 1885

November 9th

Mr. Henry T. Roberts was appointed Town Clerk at the first council meeting.

November 9th

After the meeting of the newly-elected Town Council, the Mayor, Ald. Thomas M. Wescott, provided a banquet in the Town Hall. Invitations were limited to the members of the Corporation and of the old Local Board. At 7 pm people from the town and district began to assemble in the Market Place, where the Wokingham Brass Band was playing. Fireworks were let off and there were various entertainments. At 8 pm there was a torchlight procession led by the band, Afterwards there was a bonfire on Langborough Recreation Ground and a display of fireworks. Over 2,000 people were present.

Thomas Manley Wescott (1830-1916), Wokingham's First Mayor

November 14th

It was reported that as second election would be held on 23rd November to choose four Councillors to fill the places of Messrs. Wescott, Goodchild, Moorcock and Martin who had been elected Aldermen. It was noted that seven of the candidates unsuccessful on 9th November would be nominated again, and a number of new candidates were expected to enter the field.

November 23rd

The Municipal Election to fill the four vacancies in the Town Council, held because of the appointment of four of its members to the position of

1886 - 1886

Alderman, took place at the Town Hall. There were nine candidates. Those elected were: Daniel Norton Heron (202); Robert Henderson (174); George Sale (167); Frederick Johnson (153).

December 7th

It was resolved to invite John Walter III to be High Steward of the Borough. Mr. Ducrocq was appointed Assistant Treasurer at a salary of £10. The Town Clerk's salary was fixed at £75 per annum.

1886

A footbridge was built over the railway line following two accidents at the level crossing in Barkham Road.

February

Whilst men working for the Wokingham Corporation were digging gravel on the Glebe land, small quantities of broken Roman and other ancient pottery were discovered at a depth of about four feet.

April

Mr. H. Hutt of Reading attended the Council meeting and stated that he was willing to rent the Market for the sole right of sale by auction at a rental of £10 per annum for three years, at the end of which time, if he wished, the agreement would be extended for four years. Mr. Hutt's proposal was accepted.

Wokingham Market

1887 - 1887

April 20th

A new Fortnightly Auction Market was formally opened by the Mayor of Wokingham.

1887

January 4th

Because of adverse weather conditions work in the Wokingham district was hard to come by and this caused considerable distress. A soup kitchen was started at the British Workman, a working men's club in Peach Street, and quantities of soup were distributed to the public.

April 2nd

The foundation stone of the Queen's Jubilee Almshouses in Peach Street was laid by Miss Mary Ann Shorter on behalf of her aunt, the Mayoress, Mrs. Wescott, who was indisposed.

April 13th

William and Gunhilda, the son and daughter-in-law of Joseph Brown, Rector of St. Paul's Church, Wokingham, were drowned when their ship, the S. S. Victoria, ran aground off Dieppe in France in thick fog. Their bodies were later recovered.

William Towers Brown (1858-1887)
Gunhilda Mary (1864-1887)

May 25th

William and Gunhilda were buried in the churchyard of St. Paul's, Wokingham.

1887 - 1887

June 21st

The people of Wokingham celebrated Queen Victoria's Golden Jubilee by opening the Queen Victoria Almshouses in Peach Street. Dinner was also served to 1,100 Wokingham residents in the Market Place and the name of Rose Street was changed to Queen Street.

Queen Victoria Almshouses

September 20th

A fire occurred at Old Warren Farm, the property of Lord Braybrooke, situated near Bill Hill, Billingbear and Wokingham. It was believed that the fire was the work of an arsonist who had taken advantage of the darkness and wind to create the greatest damage.

December

John Walter III accepted the position of High Steward of Wokingham

John Walter III (1818-1894)

1889 - 1890

1889

March 6th

Wokingham Cyclists' Club was formed at Symonds' Bank. The members intended to arrange runs on Wednesday evenings during the summer.

August 14th

The Wokingham Cyclists' Club held their first illuminated ride. Twenty cyclists met at the Rose Hotel and paraded along the main streets captained by Mr. Arthur Heelas. The cycles were decorated with Chinese lanterns and fairy lights.

November 9th

At the Mayor's Banquet the Mayor, Cllr. William Moorcock, was invited to take up the matter of providing a swimming pool for the public of Wokingham during his year of office. He promised to consider the matter.

December

At a meeting of agriculturalists and others it was decided to form a Sparrow Club for the neighbourhood in the interests of agriculture. 4½d. per dozen birds killed was offered for sparrows and other birds that destroyed crops.

1890

Miss Laura Baker and her sister Lucy opened *The Retreat* school in Milton Road.

Miss Laura Jane Baker (1868-1953)

1891 - 1891

September 31st

After being closed for repairs the Milton Road Baptist Chapel was re-opened. The Rev. J. Cave, the pastor, preached both in the morning and in the evening.

1891

January

Without explanation from this month onwards the Lending Library in Wokingham Town Hall was no longer mentioned in Parish Magazine notices. Presumably the library was closed.

January

The Wokingham Cyclists' Club took over the premises of the Wokingham Working Men's Club in Peach Street, for use as a club house. The W.W.M.C. at that time was practically defunct. The Wokingham Cyclists' Club then amalgamated with the Wokingham Working Men's Club under the title of The Wokingham Cyclists' Club.

April 21st

The new steam fire engine expressly built for the Wokingham Voluntary Fire Brigade by Merryweather & Son, of London arrived. The thirty horse power engine was capable of sending water to a height of 150 feet with a working pressure of 100 lbs. Four distinct hose jets could be used. After the trials the new steam fire engine was christened *Alert* by Mrs. Murdoch, wife of the M.P. for Reading.

Steamer fire engine Alert
drawn by Tilling Greys,
Dolly and Dustpan

1892 - 1892

June 17th

A sale of goods and work, at an "American Fair," took place at Highfield, Milton Road, the residence of Commissioner Gregorie. The was well attended, especially at the clothing and tea stalls. Nearly everything was sold.

June 17th

A bicycle race took place under the auspices of the Wokingham Cycling Club. The selected route began from the *Two Poplars* Inn to the letter-box at Finchampstead and back, a distance of almost five miles. There were 15 starters, the race being against time and handicapped, two competitors leaving the starting point together. The three winners were: F.J. Wells 1 (18m. 10s., allowed 2m); R. Simmons 2 (18m. 12s, allowed 1m.); W. Scribbens 3 (17m. 20s.).

June 23rd

The Volunteer Fire Brigade received a telephone call from Bearwood mansion asking them to attend a fire. As the new steam engine was being prepared the brigade received another call stating that their services would not be required. A third message was then received requesting the brigade to come as quickly as possible. On arrival at Bearwood the firemen found the engine shed adjoining the mansion to be on fire. The steamer soon extinguished the flames, and the fire was confined to the building.

June 20th

To mark the anniversary of the accession of Queen Victoria. Flags were flown from the Town Hall, the Drill Hall and other places in the town.

1892

March

Members of The Wokingham Cyclists' Club decided to leave the Peach Street premises because one of the conditions of the agreement of the occupancy of the rooms stated that no intoxicants should be served in the rooms. It was agreed with the landlord, the Rev. E. Sturges of All Saints' Church, that notice to surrender tenancy at Christmas would be served.

1892 - 1892

September 26th

The Wokingham Company of the Boys' Brigade was formed by the Rev. E. C. Leslie, Curate of St. Paul's Church, who became Captain. The company was inaugurated in the Terrace Room at a meeting for boys only and, when the object of the Brigade was explained, 80 boys joined.

The 1st Wokingham Company Boys' Brigade
Courtesy Mrs. Joy Barnes

November

It was announced that The Wokingham Cyclists' Club had accepted the offer of premises in Denmark Street by Joseph Dearlove, plumber.

November 10th

At a special general meeting of The Wokingham Cyclists' Club it was decided to rename the Club The Wokingham Club.

November 25th

Her Majesty's Buck-hounds met in the Market-place. A deer, which was taken by cart and released in a meadow belonging to Mr. R. Green, immediately ran in the direction of Binfield. Eventually it returned to Wokingham and, crossing the playground of St. Paul's Schools, made for the Station and was eventually captured near the Market Place.

1893 - 1893

December 5th

The Wokingham Club opened their new rooms in Denmark Street. After Mr, Charles T. Murdoch of Buckhurst declared the Club opened the Mayor, Cllr. William White, presented Mr. Murdoch with an enlarged photograph of himself on behalf of the Club.

1893

January 10th

William James Chalmers (b. 1st. Aug. 1824) died and was buried in All Saints' Churchyard. He had served as Sergeant-at-Mace for 25 years, as well as being hall keeper and toll collector. The office of Sergeant-at Mace had been held by members of the same family for upwards of a hundred years.

May 25th

A mayor's chain, badge and robe, paid for by public subscription, were presented to the Mayor by John Walter III, High Steward, at a banquet held in the Town Hall.

June 24th

The illuminated clock, donated by John Walter III and installed in the tower attached to St. Paul's Schools, was started for the first time at 12.30 p.m.

July 20th

St. Paul's Parish Room, clock tower and extra school rooms at the junction of Station and Reading Roads were officially opened by John Walter III.

St. Paul's clock tower and school

courtesy Mrs. Joy Barnes

1894 - 1894

1894

June 28th

A special meeting was held at which the Surveyor was instructed to proceed with a new drain to carry off the surface water from Station Road and Barkham Road. Instructions were also given for an inspection of shop window blinds with a view to requiring them to be raised to the prescribed height.

July

A special notice was issued by the Water Company during the week to consumers stating that, "Owing to the present drought the directors find it necessary to cut off the supply during the hours from twelve at noon till six o'clock in the morning."

July 25th

The Ancient Order of Foresters, Wokingham, held their annual rural fete in a meadow in Wellington Road, kindly lent by Mr. William T. Martin. The members of the club started in procession from the Court House and paraded through the town at midday, led by the Town Band.

August 18th

By order of the County Council the part of the parish of Wokingham located within the Urban Sanitary District became a separate parish called the parish of Wokingham Within. The part outside the Urban Sanitary District became the parish of Wokingham Without.

November 3rd

John Walter III, 13th High Steward of Wokingham, died and the position of 14th High Steward devolved to his eldest son Arthur Fraser Walter.

Arthur Fraser Walter (1846-1910)

1895 - 1896

1895

January

The offer of the Mayor, Cllr. George T. Philips, to donate new dials and the necessary apparatus for illuminating the Town Hall clock, provided the Corporation would undertake future maintenance, was unanimously accepted.

July 13th

The traffic through Wokingham came to a standstill because a cow being driven through the town had escaped and all attempts to capture it had failed. The borough water cart was backed towards the animal and the water turned on, but the cart was charged again and again. Other cows were brought to the scene and the infuriated animal joined them. It was eventually led to a nearby meadow.

November 24th

A large storehouse belonging to Messrs. Isaiah Gadd and Co., Ltd, in Finchampstead Road, near the Corporation Gas Works, together with some cottages, caught fire. The Brigade was called at 7 pm when many of the firemen were either at church or chapel, but they arrived promptly. Their united efforts eventually subdued the blaze.

1896

January

The unanimous resolutions passed at the meetings of the Basingstoke and Wokingham Urban District Councils conclusively proved the popularity of the project to join Basingstoke and Wokingham by a direct railway line which would not only form the connecting link between the main line of the London and South Western Railway and the Staines and Wokingham Branch, but would also be of great advantage to the intermediate district. Reading, Basingstoke and Wokingham markets would be opened up to tenant farmers, who would be able to sell their produce without having to cart their wares over long distances by road.

1897 - 1897

February 21st

A public meeting was held in Wokingham Town Hall to discuss the proposed new railway between Wokingham and Basingstoke.

November 11th

Some pupils of the Palmer Schools celebrated a perfect two-year attendance record.

Pupils of the Palmer Schools celebrating a perfect two-year attendance record

December 26th

The following article appeared in the Reading Mercury: *Wokingham was aroused on Tuesday morning by the appearance of a motor car which was driven through the town from the direction of Bracknell towards Reading.*

1897

June 19th--22nd

In addition to planning the public festivities for Queen Victoria's Diamond Jubilee the Council started two funds. The first was for the maintenance of a nurse to provide the country section of the parish of Wokingham with the same medical facilities that had been provided for the

1897 - 1897

town for several years. The second was for the construction of a nurse's home as a permanent memorial building. An illuminated address was also sent to the Queen.

The Mayor and Mayoress received the inmates of the almshouses as their guests and, at midnight, a peal from the tower of All Saints' Parish Church announced the completion of sixty years of the Queen's reign.

Early on Sunday morning the bells rang and, shortly afterwards, the Mayor and dignitaries paraded to All Saints' Parish Church to attend a service of thanksgiving.

Next day an ox, donated by Mr. Ifould, Captain of the fire brigade, was roasted by members of the fire brigade in the Market Place. After cooking all night, the ox was declared at noon to be ready for consumption. At lunchtime nearly a thousand people received a Jubilee Plate.

Diamond Jubilee festivities in the Market Place

Later that afternoon approximately 1,150 children assembled at the west end of Broad Street and sang the National Anthem and *All People That on Earth do Dwell*. At Langborough Recreation Ground sports were provided and, in the evening, there was a singing competition in the Market Place that lasted until nearly midnight.

1898 - 1898

1898
The Emmbrook Cricket Club was formed.

March

Wokingham Council accepted a painting of Prince George of Denmark offered by Miss Penny on behalf of her brother, the Rev. C. W. Penny.

May 18th

Batty's Barn Farm estate, consisting of fifty-seven acres of land and several cottages, which had been the property of the late Mr. James Skerritt and his family for many years, was put up for auction at the Rose Hotel by Mr. J.J. Cooper of the firm of Messrs J. Omer Cooper.

July

Appearing before the Mayor, Cllr. Daniel N. Heron, William Green was sent to prison for refusing to break stones at the Workhouse. A similar penalty was imposed on John Smith, another vagrant, for begging in Easthampstead Road.

July 26th

When Mr. Henry Bowyer and his wife were driving downhill by St. Paul's Schools the horse fell and Mr. and Mrs. Bowyer were thrown out of the cart. Mrs. Bowyer's face was badly cut and she was taken to a nearby house.

August

Wokingham Corporation resolved to draw the attention of the Right Hon. Secretary of State for War to the fact that Her Majesty's soldiers and horses could be billeted in the town they halted in, when marching, at the present schedule of prices. They respectfully asked that these prices be raised so that ratepayers would not lose money by providing this accommodation.

September 8th

The "Magpies" were asked by the Wokingham Football Club to take over the management of the Club. They decided to do so and in future they would be known as the Wokingham Football Club.

1899 - 1900

December 5th

A robbery took place on Monday night at the *Roebuck* in the Market Place. It appears that at about 9.40 p.m. a supposed commercial traveller drove up to the inn in a pony trap and asked for accommodation for the night. On the following morning the man ordered breakfast and stated that he had business at the Post Office, and would return soon. When he failed to do so suspicion was aroused, and it was found that he had left. Apparently he booked a ticket to Bracknell station on the 9.58 a.m. train but did not travel by rail. Instead he hired a fly at the Railway Hotel and drove to Reading. As a result no trace of him was found.. The pony and trap were left at an inn in Reading and were later recovered by their rightful owner. The stolen property included a considerable sum in gold, bank notes and jewellery.

1899

January 16th

The fire brigade were called to Mr. Newsome's house in Peach Street where a fire had broken out in an upstairs room in which there were empty packing cases and surplus furniture. The fire brigade were successful in extinguishing the flames before much damage was done.

February 20th

A successful smoking concert was held at Wokingham Club House under the Chairmanship of the Mayor. More than 66 members were present.

November 2nd

The first two planning applications to build houses on Batty's Barn Estate were approved. The first was submitted by Miss Violet Shewell Morris for a house in Murdoch Road. The second was for a house named *Meadowcroft* in Crescent Road, the application being made by the People's Investment Company, which retained ownership for several years.

November 14th

A grand patriotic concert, under the patronage of Prince and Princess Christian in aid of the Widows and Orphans of soldiers and sailors killed in the War, was held in the Drill Hall, Wokingham. The Princess was President and a founder member of the Red Cross.

1900 - 1900

1900

The main sewers were laid in Rose Street.

February 27th

Twenty men of the Wokingham Company of Berkshire Volunteers were given a send-off in the Drill Hall before departing for South Africa. A dinner was provided in the Drill Hall and Mrs. Allfrey of Ashridgewood gave a pocket compass to each soldier.

March 1st

The news of the Relief of Ladysmith was received with great enthusiasm on Thursday morning and in a very short time Wokingham was decorated with flags and banners. A peal was rung on the bells of All Saints Church and a salute of twenty-one fog signals was fired at the Railway Station. At night there was a torchlight procession in which the town band, the Volunteer Band, the Fire Brigade and Boys' Brigade took part.

May 7th

On Monday evening Privates Clacy, Musto and Gough, members of the Wokingham Company of Berkshire Volunteers, were given a send-off by their comrades and townspeople. Sergt. Benstead organised a smoking concert at the Bush Hotel, at which Dr. Hessman presided, and a large company attended. Mrs. Alfrey of Ashridgewood gave the three members a pocket compass, and the past and present members of the company gave them each a watch.

May 21st

The Relief of Mafeking was celebrated on Monday evening. The Mayor issued a handbill announcing a torchlight procession and inviting the inhabitants to decorate and illuminate their houses. Flags, buntings and Chinese lanterns were displayed from almost every house in the Borough. The procession was timed to start at 10 pm but long before that time the streets were crowded with people, and a great number of fireworks were discharged.

October 8th

A room in Station Road was provided for the headquarters of the Rifle Club. It was intended to open the room on Mondays, Wednesdays and

1901 - 1902

Fridays from 7.30 to 9.30 pm and on Wednesday afternoon from 3.00 to 5.00 o'clock.

1901

Mr. T. W. Walker, a former member of the Wokingham Company of Berkshire Volunteers, died from enteric fever in South Africa. Before volunteering to go to South Africa he had been employed in Wokingham Post Office.

January 22nd

Queen Victoria died at Osborne House on the Isle of Wight.

February 2nd

Prince Albert Edward, Prince of Wales, was proclaimed King Edward VII. The Proclamation was read by the Mayor, Cllr. Edwin C. Hughes, from a platform that had been erected outside the Town Hall. Despite the bad weather a large crowd of people filled the Market Place.

March 31st

According to the Census, the inhabitants of the Parish of Wokingham numbered 6002, an increase of 688 since the last one.

June 21st

The men of the Wokingham Company of Berkshire Volunteers were welcomed home from South Africa with a public dinner held in the Drill Hall.

July 11th

Mrs. W. Howard Palmer laid the foundation stone of the new Church House in Easthampstead Road for All Saints Parish Church Wokingham.

October 30th

The Active Service members of the Wokingham Company of Berkshire Volunteers were presented with travelling clocks in Wokingham Town Hall in recognition of their service in South Africa.

1902

The Garth Hunt's name was adopted to mark the retirement of Mr. Thomas Colleton Garth, who had been Master since 1852.

1902 - 1902

The Primitive Methodists built a Sunday School next to their chapel at the bottom of Denmark Street.

The first town sub post office was opened at No.6 Barkham Road near the railway station under Benjamin Kirby, proprietor of the grocery store.

Lime trees were planted in Broad Street.

June 11th

The people of Wokingham celebrated the conclusion of the South African War with a torchlight procession through the streets led by the band of the Wokingham Company of Berkshire Volunteers. A large bonfire was lit by the Mayoress and there were fireworks on Langborough Recreation Ground.

June 26th

Because of the King's illness all preparations for the celebration of the Coronation in Wokingham were immediately suspended. It was later decided that, in accordance with the King's wishes, on Thursday, June 26th (the original date of the Coronation) dinner would be served to the poor and the children's tea would be held. At the conclusion of the tea the children marched to the end of Broad Street where the National Anthem was sung, and three cheers were given for the King and Queen and the Mayor and Mayoress.

July 11th

All Saints' Church House was formally opened by Herbert Benyon, Lord-Lieutenant of the County.

All Saints' Church House

1903 - 1903

August 9th

The Coronation of Edward VII and his wife Alexandra took place.

November 19th

The Marquis of Downshire, of Easthampstead Park, was fined £3 for driving a motor car at a greater speed than twelve miles per hour.

1903

1903 was a time of secularisation in France and Roman Catholic schools were being forced to close down. Mère Joseph, Mother General of the Congregation at Tours in France, started looking abroad to open new missions. Through the intermediary of a Miss Johnston who lived in Ascot, the Sisters were asked to come to Wokingham to start a school for poor Irish immigrants who lived in the neighbourhood.

January 24th

The first issue of the Wokingham and Bracknell Gazette & County Review, the predecessor of the Wokingham Times, was published. The founder was Francis Staniland, a missionary returned from Japan, who was horrified that the town did not have its own newspaper. The Gazette was printed on a press in the basement of Clark and Son, a small grocer's shop in Market Place, later the International Stores. The newspaper offices and premises remained there until 1931. The newspaper went through several changes of name - see Appendix for full list of changes.

August

Wokingham Town Council's offer of £1,500 for the purchase of the Police's interest in Wokingham Town Hall was accepted.

October

French Sisters Edmée and Sr. Théophane were sent to Wokingham to open a school and chapel. After searching for a suitable building, they selected a large house at No. 21 Market Place which they considered *une jolie et grande maison.*

Wokingham School and Chapel
© Wokingham Convent

1904 - 1905

November

The County Police Committee purchased some land from Mr. Philip Sale at the corner of Milton and Rectory Roads to be used as a site for the new police station.

1904

A gospel hall, later to become the Salvation Army citadel, was built in Sturges Road.

The Wokingham Market was revived by Thimbleby and Shorland of Reading who held the tenancy until 1918.

Work commenced to build the police station designed by Joseph Morris, the County Architect, in Rectory Road. The builder was Messrs Edwin C. Hughes.

January

The Wokingham and Bracknell Gazette and County Review became the Wokingham, Bracknell and Crowthorne Gazette and Sandhurst News.

January 18th

The first Catholic school and chapel for the poor Roman Catholic children of Wokingham was opened.

February 14th

The Bishop of Portsmouth, the Rev. Cahill came to bless the Roman Catholic community.

February 28th

Captain Sir Edward Walter K.G.B. (b. 1824), founder of the Corps of Commissionaires, died. He was buried at Bearwood..

1905

Mr. Guglielmo Marconi visited Wokingham and lunched at the Rose, lavishing great praise on Mrs. Churchman, the wife of the proprietor, for the "splendid menu".

January

The Wokingham, Bracknell and Crowthorne Gazette and Sandhurst

1906 - 1906

News became the Wokingham, Bracknell and Crowthorne Gazette and East Berks Advertiser.

June

The police moved into the new police buildings in Rectory Road.

Wokingham Police Station

September

Palmer School formed a School Cadet Company to teach discipline, obedience, musketry, loyalty, patriotism and pride.

1906

The Salvation Army returned to Wokingham and opened a chapel in Rose Street.

January 8th

Wescott Road Council Schools in Goodchild Road were formally opened by Mrs. Murdoch, wife of the M.P. for Reading. They were named after Thomas Manley Wescott, the first Mayor of Wokingham.

May 24th

On Empire Day the children of the elementary schools of Wokingham were given a holiday. Flags were hoisted on the Town Hall and other buildings. Special reference was made in the schools to the life and work of Queen Victoria, and the progress of the Empire during her long and prosperous reign.

1907 - 1909

June

When the Convent lease in the Market Place expired the Convent was moved to *Bartons* in Crescent Road for six months.

December

Wokingham Town Football Club moved from Langborough Road grounds to grounds in Finchampstead Road.

December 20th

The Convent moved again to No. 73 Easthampstead Road, the last house in town. The stables were converted to form the Chapel.

1907

February 8th

Col. Arthur Fraser Walter opened a miniature rifle range on The Terrace, donated by Cllr. Thomas Edward Ellison for use by army cadets.

1909

A Mr. Farbrother, a journeyman carpenter, built an airship in a large shed in Easthampstead Road. His project aroused considerable interest and local people subscribed a large amount of money. The *Wokingham Whale*, as the ship was called, appears never to have been completed.

The Wokingham Whale
courtesy Wokingham Times

1910 - 1910

February

Wokingham Savings Bank was opened in the Town Hall.

1910

The Primitive Methodist Chapel in Denmark Street closed down because of a decline in attendances.

February 5th

A local band of ringers succeeded in ringing a true complete peal of grandsire triples at St. Paul's Church. It was the first ever rung in Wokingham.

February 22nd

Arthur Fraser Walter, 14th High Steward of Wokingham died.

May 6th

King Edward VII died. He was succeeded by his younger brother, Prince George Frederick Ernest Albert, who became King George V.

May 12th

Residents of Wokingham assembled outside the Town Hall at noon to hear the proclamation of his Majesty King George V.

July

Miss Ann Creaker bequeathed an oil painting of the late Mr. Thomas Creaker, who was several times alderman, to Wokingham Town Hall.

September 28th

The New Wokingham Club premises at No. 21 Market Place, Wokingham were formally opened, with some 200 guests present. The Mayor and Mayoress, Mr and Mrs. William Howard Palmer, and Mr. Denis Frederick Denis de Vitré, member, and his wife were on the platform.

New Wokingham Club premises

1911 - 1911

1911

Rates were reduced to 6s 4d in the pound.

March

The census revealed the population of Wokingham to be 7,686, an increase of 1,684 in a decade.

March 25th

Thomas Edward Ellison, Parish Church Warden, purchased St. Paul's School and clock tower from the Walter family and donated them to the Parish of St. Paul.

March 28th, 29th & 30th

The particulars and plans of the sale of 124 lots of freehold properties comprising the outlying portions of the Bearwood Estate, were issued. The dates of the sale were fixed for Tuesday, Wednesday, and Thursday, March 28th, 29th and 30th at the Drill Hall, Wokingham. The lots comprised properties in the parishes of Wokingham, Arborfield, Barkham, Newland, Finchampstead, Sandhurst, Winnersh, and Yateley, extending in all to about 3,240 acres.

May 21st

A new Roman Catholic Church at The Terrace, Wokingham, was formally opened, having been privately blessed on the previous day.

The new Roman Catholic Church
© Wokingham Convent

1911 - 1911

May 30th

The Rector of St. Paul's Parish Church presented Thomas Edward Ellison with a silver casket as a token of gratitude from St. Paul's parishioners in recognition for donating St. Paul's Schools to the parish. It is now known as the Ellison Casket.

The Ellison Casket

June 22nd

The Town's celebrations for the Coronation of George V and Queen Mary included special church services, a fete and gymkhana at Starmead and an ox roast and a dinner of two sittings at the Town Hall for 700 of the elderly.

1912 - 1913

August

Arthur Hill (1872-1918)

Arthur Wills John Wellington Blundell Trumbull Hill, 6th Marquis of Downshire, was appointed 15th High Steward of Wokingham.

1912

Public toilets were installed in the Town Hall.

March 11th

Under the auspices of the National Union of Women's Suffrage Societies a meeting was held at the Studio, Great Mead, Wokingham.

July 10th

The general competition of the South Midland District of the National Fire Brigades Union, and general sports were held in a large field off Easthampstead Road, Wokingham

1913

The Borough Council awarded prizes for the best allotments.

Land was purchased from the Walter Estate for the Barkham Recreation Ground and Ormonde Road Allotments.

Wokingham Brewery in Broad Street closed.

1914 - 1914

March 10th

The Mayor, Cllr. William T. Martin, formally opened the *Electric Theatre* in Broad Street and switched on the first film entitled *His Lordship, the Valet.*

The Electric Theatre
courtesy Wokingham Times

1914

August 4th

The First World War began when Great Britain declared war with Germany.

August 20th

A meeting was held in Wokingham Town Hall to enable Colonel Carter to give some information about the calling up of extra men.

August 31st

Wokingham Voluntary Fire Brigade's first motorised fire engine BL 035 was delivered. The Dennis patent turbine motor fire engine was ordered from the makers at Guildford; the engine was from 40 to 45 horsepower; had 1,200 feet of hose and a 60 foot jet, and was capable of travelling 30 miles an hour. The price was £725 and the fire engine was christened *Swift*.

1915 - 1915

Fire engine Swift BL 035
courtesy Reading Mercury

September

Through the kindness of Mr. Cusack, Shute End House was loaned for Belgian refugees. The furniture was borrowed from some of the residents of Wokingham and the house had been thoroughly cleaned.

October 21st

A social evening and whist drive was held in the Drill Hall on Wednesday evening in aid of the Tobacco fund for the 1st and 2nd Battn. Royal Berks Regiment at the front. There was a good attendance.

November 13th

Some forty-five special constables were sworn in before Cllr. Henry C. Mylne and Mr. L. R. Erskine. Each was to be given a warrant card, which had to be carried at all times, and they were to be kitted out with a staff, whistle and badge. Their work was to prevent sabotage by enemy agents.

1915

Edward Farnell, grocer at Emmbrook opened a sub post office.

January 31st

Church House was converted into a temporary military hospital by the Red Cross Voluntary Air Defence.

1915 - 1915

February 9th

Large numbers of townspeople assembled on Tuesday to give a send off to the 10th Battalion Northumberland Fusiliers and the Durham Light Infantry who had been billeted in Wokingham for a short time. The Colonel of the Durhams called for three cheers from his men for "the kindly people of Wokingham."

March 11th

An organ recital was given in the evening by Mr. H. Roscoe Eady, F.R.C.O., to a large congregation in All Saints' Parish Church. The collection was for funds to provide recreation huts at the British Base Camps in France.

March 20th

Some 2,000 men, with 60 officers, of the 5th Berks and the 7th Norfolks marched into the town to their billets, which they would occupy for ten days. The men looked particularly fit after their march from Aldershot and their skirmishing from Eversley.

May

Mrs. Dunne of Toutley Hall organised a scheme for the collection of eggs in the district for the wounded at the front.

June 9th

Fifteen wounded soldiers arrived from the front at Easthampstead Road War Hospital. The hospital up until then had been used for the treatment of minor cases for troops in the district.

June 28th

The town was visited by a detachment of the Royal Berkshire Regiment under the command of Major Tennyson D'eyncourt to encourage recruiting. They were met at the borough boundary, Easthampstead Road, by Major Denis de Vitré, local recruiting officer, and the Mayor of Wokingham, Ald. Henry C. Mylne, accompanied by the Town Clerk, Mr. Clifton, and the sergeant-at-mace.

August

At the invitation of the Walter family Bearwood mansion was taken over by the Canadian Government for use as a military convalescent hospital.

1916 - 1916

September 20th

Bearwood Canadian Convalescent Hospital was opened and Major Robert Wodehouse, Officer Commanding, arrived on the following day.

The Canadian Military Hospital

December 21st

One thousand one hundred and sixty-four new-laid eggs in addition to the weekly collection were sent from the Wokingham District Depot as a Christmas gift and expression of gratitude to wounded soldiers.

1916

Women and girls were required to work on the land since most of the able male population were at war. Others cycled as far as Farnborough to work on aircraft engines.

February

The Town Hall War Work Party was recognised as a Branch of the Berkshire Association of Voluntary Organisations.

1917 - 1917

May

The Wokingham Food Production Association was formed by Cllr. Henry Mylne, Mayor of Wokingham.

August

The pupils at Palmer School, by each contributing one penny, were able to send parcels to two old boys—Privates Arthur Gasson and William Band—who were prisoners of war.

September

Miss Sally Gadd, owner of Montague House, gave permission for the building to be used as a club for troops.

December 19th, 20th

A very successful sale of work organised by the Mayoress's working party was held in the Town Hall. It was originally intended to hold the sale on Tuesday only but, owing to its success, it was decided to continue for a second day. The takings totalled upwards of £126.

1917

March 28th

The staff at Miss Baker's (Grosvenor House) School gave a concert in the schoolroom in aid of huts for women munitions workers.

March 28th

A lecture in the Town Hall by Mr. Jones was well attended. Advice was given on the sowing of carrots, turnips, broccoli etc., but the lecturer strongly advised all present to concentrate their principal efforts on providing food for winter use.

1918 - 1918

April

The members of the Local War Savings Committee distributed a large number of pledge cards in the town. The cards indicated a commitment by the holder to save. Above the pledge was the King's Proclamation. A narrow purple ribbon was selected by the National Committee to be worn on the edge of the coat by those who had signed the pledge cards, as a symbol of adherence to the principle of voluntary rationing.

April 11th

In connection with the Wokingham Women's Meeting a tea and social was given in the schoolroom of the Wesleyan Church to fifty wounded Canadian Soldiers from Bearwood Hospital. A gramophone lent by Cllr. W. Bodle added to the pleasure of the tea.

April 20th

The American flag was first flown together with the Union Jack from Wokingham Town Hall in recognition of the entry of America into the war.

September 13th

A welcome was given to thirty-four Canadian soldiers when they arrived at Wokingham to recuperate after having been German prisoners-of-war.

1918

Luckley School was founded in 1918. The main house, which dated from 1907, had replaced Luckley Manor House, an ancient property mentioned in the Domesday Book.

The 1st Emmbrook Troop of Boy Scouts was started.

The Salvation Army closed its chapel in Rose Street.

A weighing machine, purchased from the Gas Works for £10 and adapted to weigh cattle, was installed outside the Town Hall.

March

The scholars of various schools in the town were encouraged to take up the cultivation of land. Allotments were secured in Sturges Road and Station Road, and work was supervised by the head masters.

1919 - 1919

March

A report of the Town Hall War Working Party showed that, in 1917, 769 pairs of hospital slippers were contributed; 1,878 knitted comforts; 413 shirts, bed-jackets, etc. Altogether over 3,800 articles were made in the year. The total amount of work done by the branch, which included Wokingham, Hurst, Twyford, and, for a few months Wargrave, was roughly 3,807 articles for 1916, and 4,913 for 1917; totalling 8,720.

May 29th

Arthur Hill, 6th Marquis of Downshire and 15th High Steward of Wokingham, died.

June

A special selling centre was opened at the Town Hall. The aim was to raise £20,000 raised by the sale of bonds and certificates. A leaflet and poster campaign was carried out.

July

The people of Wokingham exceeded the target of £20,000 by saving £30,280 6s during Wokingham War Weapons Week and earned the honour of a gun being named after the town.

September 4th

It was resolved at a meeting in the Town Hall to raise a company of army cadets at Wokingham.

November 11th

Germany signed an armistice with the allies, thus ending the First World War.

1919

Two ship owners, Sir Thomas Devitt Bt. And Sir Alfred Yarrow, purchased Bearwood mansion and 500 acres of the estate from John Walter IV and offered them to the Royal Merchant Seamen's Orphanage.

March

Wokingham Town Council accepted a portrait of Alderman Thomas Manley Wescott from his widow.

1919 - 1919

March 15th

The Canadian Convalescent Hospital, Bearwood, was closed down.

May 27th

A captured gun presented to the town arrived. It was a 120mm German howitzer and was badly damaged. The gun was captured by the 12th Division on 27th July 1917 and claimed by the 5th Royal Berks. Regiment.

July 6th

A public service of Thanksgiving for Peace was held in the Market Place.

July19th

The adults of Wokingham celebrated the end of the First World War.

July 23rd

The children of Wokingham celebrated the end of the war.

Wokingham children's celebrations

1919 - 1919

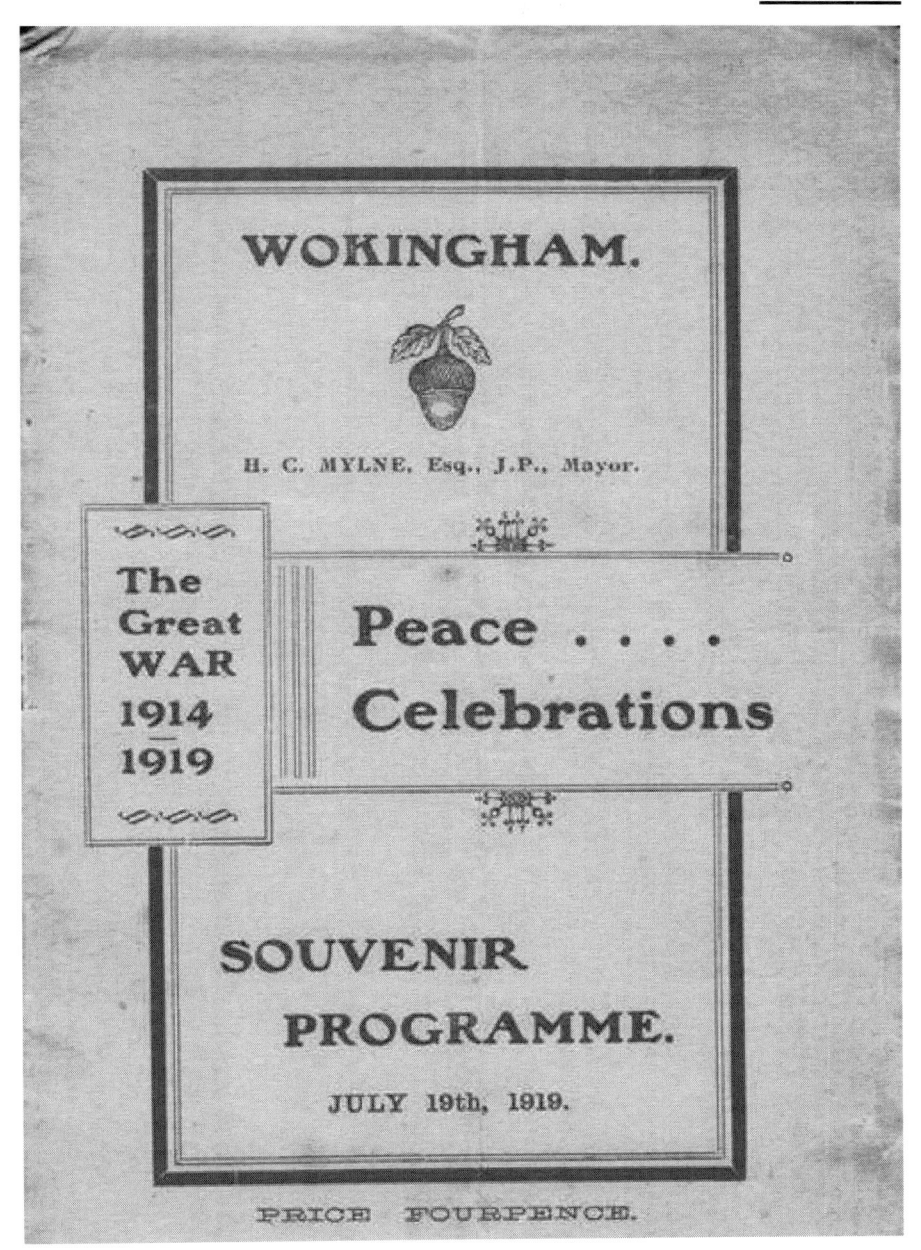

WOKINGHAM.

H. C. MYLNE, Esq., J.P., Mayor.

The Great WAR 1914–1919

Peace . . . . Celebrations

SOUVENIR PROGRAMME.

JULY 19th, 1919.

PRICE FOURPENCE.

1920 - 1921

December

H.R.H. Prince Arthur Duke of Connaught & Strathearn was appointed 16th High Steward of Wokingham.

Prince Arthur Duke of Connaught & Strathearn (1850-1942)

1920

Benches were installed outside the Town Hall and private cars were allowed to be parked in the Market Place.

Wellington Brewery in Denmark Street closed down.

October

An orthopaedic clinic was started in two rooms in Wokingham Town Hall.

November

The General Purposes Committee recommended that the shell presented to the War Savings Committee be placed in the corridor of the Town Hall. Alderman Hughes offered to supply the base.

1921

Plans for a cinema in Rose Street were approved.

Wokingham Foundry (Vulcan Engineering Works) was burnt down one Saturday afternoon while the owner was at a football match. Arson was suspected.

The Wokingham branch of the Royal British Legion was opened.

1921 - 1921

January

An inscription was fitted to the shell presented to the War Savings Committee. The timber for the stand provided by Alderman Hughes came from an 800-year-old elm tree.

War Savings Committee shell

February 23rd

A Free Church burial ground in Reading Road, Wokingham was dedicated in the presence of a large congregation.

March 1st

The opening of the Royal Merchant Navy School and the dining hall at Bearwood was performed by the Marquis of Graham and not by H.R.H. the Duke of York as was carved on the stonework.

May 24th

Empire Day was celebrated at Wokingham. In the evening the Boy Scouts and Girl Guides combined in a special parade and were inspected by the Mayor of Wokingham. The children at Palmer School joined in a special ceremony..

June 27th

A war memorial erected to commemorate the services of the men of All Saints' Parish, Wokingham, who fell in the Great War was unveiled and dedicated in a ceremony attended by a large number of townspeople.

1922 - 1923

All Saints' War Memorial was unveiled

September 4th

A memorial plaque to the men of the 'H' (Wokingham Company) 4th Batt. R.B. Regiment who fell in the war was unveiled at the Drill Hall. A roll of officers, N.C.O.s and men who mobilised or joined the company before September 18th 1914 and subsequently served overseas was also unveiled.

1922

January 22nd

A War Memorial in St. Paul's Church was unveiled and dedicated to St. Paul's parishioners who had been killed in the First World War.

Plans for an extension of the Reeves Depository in Carey Road were approved.

1923

Mr. William Latham Pick moved his Wire Rope Works from Bracknell to No. 11 Market Place, Wokingham. at the rear of the Market Place.

The Tan House, at the corner of Barkham Road and Molly Millars Lane, was closed and the site sold.

The first part of St. Theresa's Catholic Primary School was built in the Convent grounds in Easthampstead Road.

1924 - 1924

April

The Wokingham Memorial Orthopaedic Clinic was formally opened by the Marchioness of Downshire. Members of the Voluntary Aid Detachment, who assisted in the local hospitals during the war and were now identified with the work of the clinic under Commandant Lady Cayley, formed a guard of honour at the entrance hall.

Wokingham Memorial Orthopaedic Clinic

courtesy Mrs. Ann Jeater

1924

The statutes of Lucas Hospital were amended to allow the admission of married couples. Lucas Hospital was built at Chapel Green in 1665 from a bequest by Henry Lucas, to serve as an almshouse 'for the relief of old men'.

The restoration of All Saints Parish Church by Messrs Edwin C. Hughes was completed. During the restoration a skeleton, of unknown date and with a bullet in the skull, was unearthed between the south porch and chapel door.

Financier Solomon Barnato Joel (1835-1931) donated £500 to the Borough for the purchase of Holt Copse at Holt Lane.

1925 - 1925

January

Charles Goddard, Supt. Berkshire Constabulary, was included in the New Year's list of awards of the King's Police Medal. The award was one of the highest honours which could be accorded to members of the police service. He received it for his distinguished record in the administrative branches of the service, for his success in organising the Police Force, and for special services to Royalty and Heads of State.

Charles Goddard
Supt. Berkshire Constabulary (d. 1946)
courtesy Emmy Eustace

January 25th

A serious fire broke out at Mr. William Denton's warehouse near South Place off Peach Street and within an hour a double story building used by a showroom for furniture manufactured by the Forest Furnishing Company, and by Mr. Osborne as a tailor's and outfitter's shop, was completely destroyed.

September 5th

The County Council assumed the duties of the Library Authority in Wokingham and a library was opened in the bank room of the Town Hall on Fridays from 6.00 pm to 8.00 pm. The first volunteer librarian was Miss M. Harwood. There had been a slight delay in opening the library because she had broken her arm. Eventually 250 books in five boxes were dispatched by carrier to Wokingham and the library was opened.

1925

The main streets of Wokingham were cabled for electricity and many houses were connected. The power was supplied by Yorktown and Blackwater Electric Company.

1926 - 1929

1926

Electric lighting was installed in the Fire Station and Town Hall clock tower.

Mr. Jeffries displayed daily bulletins in his coal office window in the Market Place during the General Strike.

1927

The Mayoral Boards which displayed the names of Wokingham Mayors in the Town Hall were unveiled by Mrs. Wescott.

Wokingham Round Table was founded.

January

The East Berks Gazette became the Wokingham Gazette and Berkshire County Advertiser.

April

The Wokingham and District Motor Club was formed at the Bush Hotel with the hotel as its headquarters.

October 1st

The Borough of Wokingham and the Parish of Wokingham Within were extended to include part of the Parish of Wokingham Without. The number of town councillors was increased from twelve to eighteen.

1928

January 5th

Wokingham Town Football Club acquired its ground in Finchampstead Road for £900.

March

Wokingham Council agreed to sell its gas works to the company for £35,000.

1929

Mr. and Mrs. F. Lee opened a business which became the Emmbrook Post Office.

St. Theresa's School was extended to accommodate the increasing

1930 - 1930

numbers of pupils. Three downstairs classrooms in the main building became the hall and central heating was installed.

Another 17 acres of land were purchased by the Borough of Wokingham for £1,227 to add to the earlier purchase which formed the present Joel Park.

August 8th

Wokingham Bowling Club was officially founded with 36 members.

September 11th

The Wokingham Carnival was revived after a break of several years. At eight o'clock in the morning a bugle call from the Town Hall signalled the start of the festivities. The weather was perfect and the streets were thronged with people, many of whom were in fancy dress. The beating of the bounds of the enlarged borough was carried out for the first time. Many were bumped including the Mayor and Mayoress and Police Supt. Goddard. A comic cricket match was played by the ladies of the Wokingham Lawn Tennis Club and the members of the Wokingham Cricket Club. The men were handicapped by having to bat with items ranging from a beer bottle to a frying pan. The highlight was the carnival procession which included carts, motor-vans, cycles, fire engines and bands. In the evening a grand carnival ball was held at the Drill Hall.

1930

The 1st Wokingham Scout Group was founded with headquarters at No. 33 Peach Street at the rear of the Welcome Inn.

June 27th

Berkshire County Council acquired Holt Estate from the Heelas family for £7.000. The property had been unoccupied for some time.

July

In the Challenge Air Race Winifred Spooner, a Wokingham pilot, was awarded the title of *World's Champion Airwoman*; the *Gold Medal of the German Aero Club*; and the *Lufthansa Prize*, and became the first to be awarded the *Imperial Tobacco Co. Trophy* for getting the highest marks amongst British pilots in the Challenge for 1930.

1931 - 1931

October

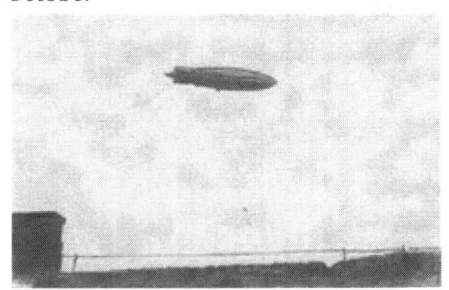

The R101, the world's largest airship, flew over Wokingham on its maiden voyage.

The R101 passing over Wokingham
Courtesy Pat Egerton

December 22nd

Winifred Spooner received a Civic Welcome at Wokingham Town Hall for saving the life of her co-pilot during her attempt to break the record of five days to fly from Croydon to Cape Town in South Africa. Winnie's aircraft crash landed in the sea off Italy and she swam two and a half miles to seek help while her co-pilot who couldn't swim sat on the wooden fuselage.

Miss Spooner stands to the right of Cllr. Dorothy Wescott
Courtesy Andrew McIrvine

1931

A council sub-committee considered plans to limit Rose Street and Peach Street to one-way traffic to ease congestion. It was decided to give this further consideration and to ask the local brewers to unload their goods by 10.00am to help the flow of traffic.

1931 - 1931

Because of financial difficulties The Wokingham & Bracknell Gazette was taken over by the General Publishing Syndicate of Bristol and the plant and offices were moved from the site in Peach Street that was later occupied by Woolworth's to a site in Emmbrook where it remained for 22 years.

Electric lighting was installed in the Town Hall by C.K. Coy.

Joel Park was created a public park.

January 15th

Wokingham County Girls' School in Holt Lane was officially opened. The first Headmistress was Miss G. M. Brown.

Wokingham County Girls' School
© The Holt School

February 13th

Reginald H. R. Palmer, president of the Wokingham Club, provided the club with a bowling green near Langborough Road to be called the Howard Palmer Bowling Green in his father's memory.

April 22nd

The change-over from the old telephone system and services to the new was made, thus completing the coming into full action of the new Post Office Buildings at the rear of the present public part of the Post Office. The new building covered an area of 3,240 square feet. The ground floor

1931 - 1931

accommodated a large sorting room and there were two rooms for the use of the P.O. engineers and linesmen. The upper floor was mainly taken up by the telephone system. The builders were Messrs. E.C. Hughes and Co., Wokingham.

May

There was no carnival that year. The money saved was to go to the Royal Berks Hospital.

May 16th

Winifred Spooner and her good friend Amy Johnson participated in a Ladies' Air Race from Woodley Aerodrome, round the spire of St. Paul's Parish Church, Wokingham, on to Twyford and back to Woodley.

The Ladies' Race" artist Geoffrey Beckett
Competitors flying over Twyford Railway Station

May 27th

The Howard Palmer Bowling Green was formally opened by Mrs. Howard Palmer, his widow.

June 10th

Wokingham Bowling Club Green, Reading Road, was formally opened by the Mayor, Alderman Albert E. Priest.

August

Saint Sebastian Parish Band was founded by the Rev. Arthur Carr, vicar of St. Sebastian's Parish Church, and the village postman Frank Every.

1932 - 1932

December 14th

Pilot Officer Douglas Robert Stewart Bader was severely injured when his aircraft crashed at Woodley Aerodrome.

1932

May 23rd.

A large combined Empire Day celebration was held at the cricket ground, Wellington Road. The Mayor, Alderman A.E. Priest, inspected the parade and afterwards took the salute, following which a hollow square was formed when, in his speech, the Mayor expressed his pleasure at being invited to the event.

July 13th

A large bomber of the "K" class, after circling in the district for some time, made a successful landing in Mr. Colebrook's field at about 4.15 p.m. A large number of people crowded into the field and the adjacent London Road.

September

Wesleyan Methodists, Primitive Methodists and United Methodists officially ceased to exist when they united to form the new Methodist Church.

September 14th

There were many stalls and events including the Crowning of the Carnival Queen which took place in the Market Place in the early afternoon, the ceremony being performed by the Mayoress, Mrs. Priest. After bouquets had been presented the Queen departed for her flower-bedecked lorry, and the Mayor, Ald. Albert E. Priest, then received his Royal Highness, the Rajah of Muckabout and some of his forty thieves. A comic football match was later played during which hockey sticks and umbrellas were frequently used. The poor referee was removed in an improvised coffin. The procession in the evening was the highlight of the day. Crowds thronged the route to see the Carnival Queen and retinue head a parade of decorated vehicles depicting various tableaux.

September 17 th

Wokingham Post Office in Broad Street, Wokingham, was formally opened by the Mayor, Ald. Albert E. Priest.

1933 - 1933

Wokingham Post Office on official opening day
courtesy Wokingham Times

1933

January

The new Social Club at Emmbrook was formally opened by the Mayor, Ald. Albert E. Priest.

January 13th

Winifred Evelyn Spooner, Wokingham's famous aviatrix and navigator died from influenza. Winnie had always been dogged by bad luck. She died on Friday 13th.

Winifred Evelyn Spooner (1900-1933)
courtesy Andrew McIrvine

1933 - 1933

June 26th

The funeral of Miss Louisa Clay took place at St. Paul's Church, Wokingham. Owing to the deceased weighing some 38 stone it was necessary to rig a derrick over the grave to lower the coffin.

September 13th

Many citizens of Wokingham entered into the spirit of the Wokingham Charity carnival by wearing fancy dress and decorating their houses and shops with flags and garlands. Despite the rain rag collectors were out in force. When the sun shone the band of the Gordon Boys' Home and the Dagenham Girl Pipers paraded the streets. Mrs. Grundy, the well-known complainer (played by a man), was soon captured and taken away.

Mrs Grundy, the complainer being taken away

October 4th

The Bishop of Oxford consecrated an addition to the burial ground at All Saints' Church, Wokingham, in the presence of a large congregation.

1934

January 16th

It was reported at a meeting of the Wokingham Hospital Committee that £1,000 had been saved by the people of Wokingham and agreed that a bed would be endowed in the Royal Berkshire Hospital.

February 18th

The Lord Lieutenant of the County, Mr. J. Herbert Benyon, president of the Royal Berkshire Hospital, accepted, in the name of its Governors, a tablet and a £1,000 endowment for the Wokingham Hospital Committee bed from Alderman A.E. Priest, President of the Wokingham Hospital Committee, through the Mayor of Wokingham, Cllr. the Rev. Charles Mansfield.

March

A meeting of the executive committee of the Wokingham Carnival was held to discuss the question of holding a carnival that year. After careful discussion it was thought advisable to postpone the event for this year and to hold the next carnival in 1935.

May 19th

The new swimming pools, constructed by Ald. William T. Martin and his son, Cathrow, behind his home, *Fernleigh*, at No. 39 The Terrace, Wokingham, were officially opened by the Mayor of Wokingham, Cllr. the Rev. Charles Mansfield.

One of Martin's pools

1935 - 1935

July 14th

A national Mark Egg Packing Station was opened at Wokingham by Alderman Albert E. Priest .

July 19th

The renovation and decoration of the clock tower, weather vane, and roof of Wokingham Town Hall commenced. The lowest tender, by Messrs. Lowe and Son, of Wellington Road, was accepted.

1935

King George V renamed the Royal Merchant Navy School, at Bearwood dropping the word *Orphanage.*

The malt house in Reading Road was sold separately from Beches Manor to the East Berks Indoor Bowling co. Ltd.

January

St. Paul's Parish Church published its first parish magazine, entitled *St. Paul's Review.*

January 16th

The rector-elect, the Rev. Viscount Mountmorres, was instituted and inducted at St. Paul's Parish Church, Wokingham.

February 4th

The annual staff social of the Wokingham Laundry Company, Ltd. was held in the British Legion Hall, Station Road. The programme included community games, dancing, songs by Miss D. Sale, monologues by Mrs. Rolf, and recitations by young Eileen Beasley.

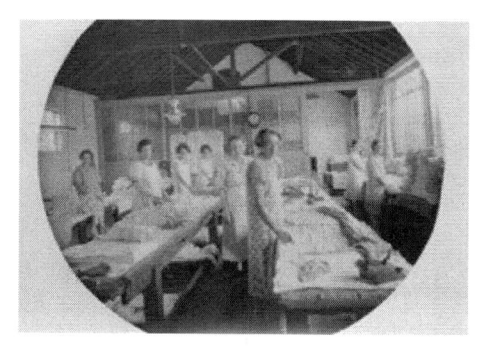

Wokingham Laundry, Station Road

1935 - 1935

May 6th

Many of Wokingham's buildings were decorated for the celebration of the Silver Jubilee of King George V. The morning began with peals of bells from All Saints' and St. Paul's Churches. Then followed a Mayoral procession from the Town Hall, down Denmark Street to Langborough Recreation Ground where the Mayoress, Miss F. Curl, planted a red maple tree. The procession then returned to the Market Place where crowds joined a United Thanksgiving Service broadcast from St, Paul's Cathedral in London. Afternoon events included sports, sideshows, tea for the children and the elderly and a concert. Dances and a firework display were held in the evening.

Borough of Wokingham

1910 to 1935

SOUVENIR PROGRAMME

OF THE CELEBRATIONS OF THE

Silver Jubilee

OF THEIR MAJESTIES

King George and Queen Mary

6th MAY, 1935

Price 1d

1936 - 1936

The Mounted Band procession in the Market Place for the Silver Jubilee

July 10th

The Annual parochial fete of St. Paul's, Wokingham, to augment the Parish and Diocesan Funds, was held at *The Elms* in Broad Street by permission of Miss Ellison. The proceedings were opened by the Mayor, Dr. Henley F. Curl, and the Rector, the Rev. Viscount Mountmorres.

October

Glebelands, off Glebelands Road, and twelve acres of grounds were presented to the Cinematograph Trade Benevolent Fund by Sir William F. Jury, president of the fund.

1936

Berkshire was removed from the diocese of Salisbury and added to that of Oxford.

A development in Peach Street, which included a Woolworth's store, commenced.

The Town Clerk received a letter from the secretary to the High Steward, the Duke of Connaught, in which he wrote, "I am directed by His Royal Highness to say that he will be pleased to have the two trees that are to be placed at the entrance of the Silver Jubilee Avenue planted in his name.

His Royal Highness also approves of the proposed avenue being named after him."

January

Generous support was given to the fund which was being raised for *Glebelands*, the Cinema Trade Benevolent Fund Home. Cheques and promises received amounted to approximately £23,000, much of which was to be spread over a period of five years, and would be largely required as capital expenditure. It was estimated that a further sum of £100,000 would be needed to produce sufficient income to endow the home permanently.

January 11th

Wokingham's new postmaster, Mr. J. T. Golothan, received a cordial welcome when the staff organised a social gathering at Wokingham Town Hall.

January 18th

As part of the Silver Jubilee celebrations the Mayor and Mayoress of Wokingham and other dignitaries planted seventy oak trees in a long avenue later named Jubilee Avenue.

January 20th

King George V died and his son Edward, Prince of Wales, ascended the throne as King Edward VIII.

January 22nd

At noon the Mayor Ald. Frederick J. Barrett read the Proclamation of his Majesty King Edward VIII to a crowded audience in the Market Place. A large platform had been erected facing Denmark Street and on it were the Mayor, the Deputy Mayor, Cllr. Henley F. Curl, the Town Clerk Mr. John H. Elliston Clifton and others.

May 5th

The Mayor, Ald. Frederick J. Barrett, on behalf of the burgesses, welcomed Superintendent Braby to the Wokingham Police Division and wished him a very successful stay in Wokingham. They were pleased to know that Superintendent Butler had practically recovered, and it was hoped that he would be spared for many years of good health in his retirement.

1936 - 1936

July 9th

Glebelands, Wokingham, Convalescent and Rest Home, was formally opened by the Lord Mayor of London, Sir Percy Vincent, at a garden party. The mansion and estate were donated by Sir William F. Jury, President of the Cinematograph Trade Benevolent Fund. The home was intended for use as a convalescent and rest home, and permanent residence for pensioners of the fund. Glebelands was built by Alfred Nicholson, designed by Ernest Newton R.A. and completed in 1897.

Glebelands Cinematograph Trade Benevolent Fund

July 9th

Ald. Philip Sale was made the first Honorary Freeman of the Borough of Wokingham.

Aldernam Philip Sale (1851-1947)

1937 - 1937

October 12th

A meeting was held in the Town Hall, convened by the Wokingham Town Council Sub-committee to inaugurate a scheme for the protection of the public in the event of air raids with chemicals, gas and fire.

October 24th

A flag day was held as part of a drive to realise a thousand pounds towards the purchase of a new fire engine for Wokingham. The Dennis engine, *Swift*, which had given good service in the area since 1914, was to be replaced by a modern vehicle.

December 5th

The death of the Rev. Viscount Mountmorres, Rector of St. Paul's Parish Church, Wokingham, occurred at Greenlands Nursing Home, Reading.

December 10th

King Edward VIII abdicated and his brother, Prince Albert, Duke of York, succeeded to the throne as King George VI.

December 14h

At noon on Monday, the Mayor of Wokingham, Ald. Frederick J. Barrett, accompanied by the Mayoress, Deputy Mayor, aldermen, councillors and officials, the clergy and representatives of public bodies, read the Royal Proclamation from a platform in the Market Place.

The Mayor, having read the Proclamation, said, "Citizens of Wokingham, I am sure that whatever regret we may have had over the happenings of last week, one thing stands out of it, over which we may well be pleased. The way in which the whole of the Royal Family have acted in this crisis has been splendid. We Wokingham people will give our loyalty unstintedly, to the new King and Queen". The Royal Merchant Navy School Band then played the National Anthem. The Mayor then said, "I call upon you to give three cheers for His Majesty King George and the Queen and one cheer for the Royal Family".

1937

February 4th

At the meeting of Wokingham Town Council it was decided to thank Mr. Arthur T. Heelas for his offer of a print of the Market Place, showing the

1937 - 1937

Old Town Hall and the old Rose Inn at Wokingham. The print was dated about 1750.

March 4th

The Mayoress of Wokingham Mrs. F. J. Barrett was the first to wear the chain and badge of office of office presented to the Council by Cllr. Miss Dorothy Wescott. The badge was purchased by her father Cllr. Thomas Manley Wescott, first Mayor of Wokingham, in 1886, as a medallion to commemorate the Golden Jubilee of Queen Victoria in the following year.

March

Canon Bertram Long, who was Rector of the parish from 1904 to 1933, published a book entitled *Records of the Parish Church and Parish of Wokingham Berks*. It contained three parts—Historical Notices starting from pre-Norman times; The Parish Church, with a description of its main features and records of many monuments of interest, and thirdly, Church Officers.

March

The daughters of the late Mr. Henry Butler presented to the Wescott School Council an interesting local collection, with the following inscription on a brass plate on the cabinet containing the collection: *Local British butterflies. Collected between 1870-1890 by Mr. Henry Butler, secretary of the British School at Wokingham from 1869-1911, and manager of the Wescott Road Council School from 1906-1932. Presented in his memory by his daughters.*

March 17th

An inquest on Tempe Irene Viscountess Mountmorres, wife of the late Viscount Mountmorres, found dead at the wheel of her car in her parents' garage, was held by the Coroner for West Surrey, Mr. G. Wills Taylor, at Farnham. The coroner returned a verdict of "Found Dead," the cause of death being carbon monoxide poisoning from the fumes of the car.

April 1st

The newly appointed Rector of St. Paul's, Wokingham, the Rev. the Hon. Patrick J. Hepburn-Scott, attended the annual vestry and parochial church meeting at St. Paul's School Room. The Rev. R. W. Tuesday, curate and priest-in-charge, presided and welcomed the new rector.

1937 - 1937

May 12th

The Coronation celebrations began with the pealing of church bells and one of the first duties undertaken by the Mayor, Cllr, Frederick Barratt, was to send a telegram of congratulation to their Majesties, King George VI and Queen Elizabeth. Children's services were held at All Saints' and St. Paul's Parish Churches. Headed by the Wokingham Town Band the Mayor and Mayoress, members of the Corporation and those of various organisations paraded to Langborough Recreation Ground where the Mayor and Mayoress each planted a Coronation oak tree. A united service was conducted in the Market Place. Balloons were later released and dancing was performed by girls from Palmer School and the 1st Wokingham Boy Scouts.

May 29th

The Union Cinemas' Ritz was opened to the public. The Mayor of Wokingham, Alderman Frederick J. Barrett J.P., presided at the opening ceremony which took place at 2.30 p.m. The first film to be shown was *Girl's Dormitory* starring Simone Simon.

The Ritz Cinema
courtesy Dusaschenka

June

The Remount Depot at Arborfield, opened in 1904 as a centre for the provision of horses for the Army, was formally closed.

June 12th

Nearly 500 children were enrolled as members of the Union Cinemas Ritz's "Chums Club". The children enjoyed a special programme of comedies, cartoons and cowboy films.

1937 - 1937

July

The cashier and commissionaire of the Union Cinemas Ritz, in full uniform were escorted through the town by a battalion of soldiers, the Wokingham Territorials, to Union Cinemas *Savoy*, where papers in connection with the film "O.H.M.S.," were picked up.

July 21st

Wokingham's new Leyland fire engine, AMO 654, which cost approximately £1,000, was delivered.

Fire engine Leyland AMO 654
courtesy Reading Mercury

September 8th

The people of Wokingham decorated the town with flags and bunting for the Coronation Carnival and many visitors came to participate in the fun. There were amusements for everyone. Children entered competitions which included skipping for girls and, for boys, eating treacle scones. Adults were invited to guess the weight of a huge lump of coal or to estimate the number of parts of a bicycle. Balloons were released by the Mayor, Cllr. Frederick Barrett, and just before two o'clock a car carried Miss Grist, the Carnival Queen, to the Market Place where she was crowned Queen by the Mayoress, Mrs. Dorothy Barrett. The Mayor then declared the fun-fair open. The carnival procession was led by a car

1938 - 1939

carrying the Mayor and Mayoress followed by the Carnival Queen and her retinue in a horse-drawn coach. The floats included a tableau of a fairy queen while another was a galley, in which were pirates played by scholars from Palmer School,

1938

Tudor Cottages at 53-61 Rose Street were demolished.

Tudor House became a doctor's surgery. It had previously been occupied by Miss Julia Maclean, milliner.

A new pavilion at Wokingham Football Ground was formally opened by Dr. Smith, a member of the Sports Committee.

January
The Railway between London and Reading was electrified.

March 26th
The first notice appeared in the *Wokingham Times & Weekly News* requesting volunteers to become members of the A.R.P. (Air Raid Precaution) Department.

June 29th
A full-time assistant Town Clerk was appointed by Wokingham Borough Council. The Town Clerk himself was still a part-time official.

July
The Wellington Arms building in Broad Street was transformed into two shops: *Felicity*, which specialised in exclusive vogues; and *Prudence*, a high-class ladies' hairdresser.

July
Voluntary Air Defence (V.A.D.) launched a mock air raid on Wokingham.

1939

The Union Workhouse, which had hitherto been a public assistance hospital, became an emergency hospital.

Wokingham's 'D' Company 11th Berks. Home Guard was formed.

1939 - 1939

The Rectory and land of St. Paul's Parish Church were sold to Wokingham Rural District Council for £3,500, to be used as Council offices.

The former Buckhurst Manor house was opened by the Sisters of Bon Secours as St. Anne's Nursing and Convalescent Home.

St. Anne's Nursing and Convalescent Home
courtesy Wokingham Times

February

Ald. William T. Martin built a splinter-proof air raid shelter, large enough to accommodate 200 people, close to his swimming pool at Wokingham.

March 29th

The first National Service rally was held in Wokingham. Processions marched through the main streets and joined forces in the Market Place. Men, women and children crowded around a platform to learn how they could do their share to strengthen the voluntary defences of the country.

1939 - 1939

April

The *Savoy* cinema re-opened after modernisation.

The Savoy Cinema

April 16th

An exercise on a more comprehensive scale than those previously attempted in the borough was carried out during the afternoon with the object of testing the communications and co-ordination of the A.R.P. services.

May 24th

The Empire Day fete was held at Tithe Barn courtesy of the Hon, Mrs. Corfield to assist the Centenary Appeals Fund of the Royal Berkshire Hospital in Reading. The stalls were arranged in the gardens and the organising committee provided a programme to attract the people of the district.

June 24th

The Bishop of Buckingham dedicated the Walter Memorial Chapel in St. Paul's Church, Wokingham. The chapel was formerly the pew of the Walters, of Bearwood. Mrs. John Walter gave permission for the conversion of the pew to complete the memorial to the Rev. Henry Walter and other members of the Walter family who had been benefactors to the church.

1939 - 1939

July

Plans were announced to purchase one acre of land for a new St. Paul's Rectory in Holt Lane.

September

A circular issued by Women's Voluntary Services for Civil Defence gave particulars to house-holders regarding the Evacuation Scheme which covered school children with teachers; children under five accompanied by their mother or a responsible adult, and expectant mothers; as well as adults who were blind and crippled.

September

The Hon. Mrs. Corfield, O.B.E. began to organise a depot for hospital supply in Wokingham at No. 3a, The Terrace. Members made bandages, operation towels and aprons, shirts, bed jackets and similar garments.

September 3rd

The Second World War began when Great Britain and France declared war on Germany.

September 8th

On Friday the Evacuation Committee received some 150 children, teachers and helpers who arrived by train. They were supplied with refreshments, and, before evening, billeted in their new homes.

September 9th and 10th

Evacuees including mothers, expectant mothers and small children arrived. The Wokingham Evacuation Committee, the members of which acted in an honorary capacity comprised: chairman: the Mayor, Cllr. James E. Thorpe; evacuation officer: Cllr. H. Lush, and secretary: Miss Harwood.

October 9th

The first meeting of the Food Control Committee of the Wokingham Rural District Council was held at the Board Room, Barkham Road, Wokingham. Mr. G. Ford, chairman, presided.

November

Wokingham's new ambulance was dedicated by the Bishop of Dorchester. It was garaged at the St. John's Ambulance Station, Eddystone Garage, Finchampstead Road.

1940 - 1940

November 3rd

A further contingent of evacuees from Battersea and Stockwell arrived in Wokingham accompanied by a number of helpers. The Mayor and the Mayoress and the secretary to the evacuation committee received them and provided refreshments in the Baptist School Room.

December 26th

The Town Hall was filled with evacuee children who were the guests of the Mayor, Cllr. Ernest Reeves. A varied programme was arranged by Mr. Percy Fuller.

1940

January 8th

Food rationing began with bacon, butter and sugar being rationed. Everyone was issued with an identity card and ration book.

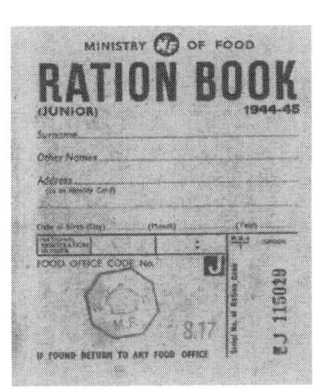

Typical identity card and ration book

January

Wokingham Rural District Council held its first meeting in the new offices at Shute End.

January 22nd

The patients of the Wokingham Public Assistance Institution were entertained to a display of operatic and tap dancing, performed by Miss Nina Kempson-Hanke and her pupils. Miss Kempson-Hanke contributed to the programme with piano solos.

1940 - 1940

March

After he had been captured by the Germans John William Gray, of the Duke of Cornwall's Light Infantry, was permitted to broadcast from a German radio station to inform his mother, who lived at Evendons Lane, Wokingham, that he was still alive and in good health.

May 14th

The Local Defence Volunteers (L.D.V.) later called the Home Guard, was formed.

June

News arrived of the first Wokingham casualties of those serving in the British Expeditionary Force.

June

Church bells were silenced and place names removed.

July

In spite of the short notice, the opening night of the Wokingham and District Rifle Club was quite successful with nearly thirty taking part in the drill, under the direction of R.S.M. Martin. Some excellent results were obtained, even by beginners.

August

Richard Been Stannard R.N.R. of Wokingham was awarded the Victoria Cross for leading two of his crew in fighting a fire on the jetty caused by a bomb igniting ammunition.

August 14th

The Mayor Cllr. Ernest W. Reeves presented each of the Wokingham men of the British Expeditionary Force, evacuated from Dunkirk, with a cigarette case containing cigarettes and a card. Each case was inscribed with the recipient's initials

1941 - 1941

August 31st

The Mayor opened the *A.B.C. Patrons and Staff Hurricane and Spitfire Fund* savings campaign at the *Ritz* cinema.

October

The Town Hall was used as a rest room for the troops during evenings.

December

The Mayor of Wokingham appealed to the people of Wokingham and District to put their binoculars on active service. There were many people who possessed field glasses but, whether their binoculars were in use or not, it was considered to be the patriotic duty of every owner to offer them to the Government.

1941

An aerial torpedo fell on the Plantation, now the site of St. Crispin's School.

January

In recognition of his association with the Wokingham Volunteer Fire Brigade for half a century, Mr. Weston B. Martin, chief officer of the brigade, was presented in the Wokingham Council Chamber with a wallet containing a cheque for £100, together with an album containing the names of the subscribers.

March 22nd

The Mayor of Wokingham, Cllr. Ernest W. Reeves, opened Wokingham's War Weapons Week by walking into the Post Office at 8.30

1941 - 1941

a.m. to purchase the first Savings Certificate. The week had already started well when one tradesman promised a gift of £500.

March 22nd-29th

The District of Wokingham more than met the challenge to save £50,000 during its War Weapons Week by saving £125,000 for the purchase of two bombers and two fighter planes. The total sum saved was £225,366.

April 8th

The Princesses Helena Victoria and Marie Louise visited the Hon. Mrs. Corfield at Tithe Barn to inspect her work as organiser of Hospital Supply Depots in Berkshire. The Queen made a similar visit on November 13th.

June 14th

As a result of the success of a Church Army canteen marquee for the Forces at Wokingham, a permanent *Pilgrim Trust* hut was erected on the same site, and was opened by Lord Darynton, president of the Church Army. The hut, which was built by the Church Army at a cost of £1,800, included a small chapel, a canteen, a stage, writing tables, games and a piano.

October 22nd

The annual meeting of the Women's British Legion, Wokingham, was held at "Mertonford," by permission of Col. And Mrs. Anderson. It was stated that 137 garments had been dispatched to the R.A.F. Comforts Fund, 46 to the Royal Navy Depot, 111 to the Army Comforts Fund, Reading, 59 to the Berks County Collecting Depot, and 56 to the local Home Guard, making a total of 409 garments.

November 30th

The King approved the award of the Distinguished Flying Medal to Flight Sgt. Henry George Matthews, 236 Squadron, in recognition of gallantry and devotion to duty in the execution of air operations. Sgt. Matthews was severely wounded during combat with two Heinkels. He continued to man his turret and during the return flight and was continuously in radio communication with his base.

1942 - 1942

December

Wokingham was allotted the Destroyer HMS *Garth* for Warships Week. If the amount aimed at (£400,000) was raised to pay for building and equipping an escort destroyer Wokingham would be eligible to adopt HMS *Garth*.

HMS Garth
courtesy Wokingham Times

1942

January 16th

H.R.H. Prince Arthur, Duke of Connaught and Strathearn 16th High Steward of Wokingham, died.

February 21st-28th

The District of Wokingham participated in "Warship Week" and exceeded the target of £400,000 to pay for the building and equipping of an escort destroyer. HMS *Garth* was adopted. The model warship that headed the parade was a float constructed by Messrs. Lee & Sons, bakers, of No. 3 Denmark Street who called it their *Bring and Buy Ship*. The final sum achieved was £480, 634.

Lee's "Bring and Buy ship" during Warship Week
courtesy Wokingham Times

1943 - 1943

March

The Ministry of Food issued an immediate order prohibiting all sales of new potatoes of the 1942 crop, including potatoes in the ground. Producers who had grown crops under glass for early sale had to apply for sales licences to the Director of Potato Supplies, St. John's College, Oxford.

May 19th

The formation of the Corps of the Royal Electrical and Mechanical Engineers was authorised by Royal Warrant.

July 20th-26th

A "Tanks for Attack" Savings Campaign for Wokingham and Rural District Area commenced. The target was £220,000 and if it was achieved three tanks would bear the name of Wokingham and Rural District Area.

July

The Mayor of Wokingham was asked to make preparations for the arrival of American troops, some of whom would be billeted in Wokingham.

August 10th

The Mayor of Wokingham presided at a recruiting meeting held at the Town Hall at 7pm in connection with the formation of a Girls' Training Corps Company in Wokingham. The immediate purpose of the Training Corps was to meet the needs of the 16—18 age group. Women over the age of 18 who were willing to serve as officers of the Corps were asked to apply to the Commandant, Mrs. John Walter, at St. Catherines, Bearwood.

December

The Royal Electrical and Mechanical Engineers (R.E.M.E.) took over the former Rosemount Depot at Arborfield Garrison.

1943

A Wokingham Produce Association was founded to encourage people to grow their own food.

February

The Wokingham Town Hall paintings that had been stored for protection earlier in the war were replaced.

1943 - 1943

February

HMS *Garth* attacked a formation of German E-boats, destroying one and damaging another. A number of prisoners and one dog were taken.

Members of Garth's crew with 'captured' dog.

Members of German E-boat's crew taken prisoner

May

The captain of HMS *Garth*, Commander Southby, and the Mayor of Wokingham, Cllr. Ernest W. Reeves, exchanged commemorative plaques at Wokingham Town Hall.

replica of ship's Badge

Wokingham Town Council plaque

1943 - 1943

May

Wokingham and District Savings Committee won the Tanks for Attack Certificate in recognition of the special effort in the Tanks for Attack Campaign, which earned for the committee the privilege of naming one tank, on which appropriately inscribed plates were placed.

June 4th

The final Wings for Victory Campaign total for Wokingham and District was announced to be £439,089 made up as follows:. Wokingham Borough, £127,054; Arborfield and Newlands, £2,657; Barkham £870; Earley, £5,481; Finchampstead, £10,182; Hurst, £50,487; Remenham, £10,095; Shinfield including Spencers Wood £5,971, £17,304; Sonning, £55,227; Swallowfield, £8,925; Twyford and Ruscombe, £26,100; Wargrave, £95,346; Winnersh, £6,261; Woodley, £21,597; Wokingham Without £1,303.

June 14th

The Mayor, Ald. Edward W. Reeves, opened the British Restaurant near the Market Place. The building had accommodation for 180 diners. In accordance with the general practice of British Restaurants, every diner helped themselves from a large hatch from the kitchen with pay desk attached.

July

It was suggested that a fund should be opened at Barclays Bank, Wokingham, on behalf of the crew of Wokingham's adopted ship, HMS *Garth*. The officer commanding had been consulted and stated that often a little financial assistance which could be given to an officer or man was a real help. If a fund could be built up, the officer commanding would be able to draw on it at his own discretion without reference to anyone else. The bank manager would then advise the Mayor of Wokingham when the balance was reduced to £50 so that a further appeal could be made. It was felt that this fund would enable the residents to keep in touch with the crew, even after the war, as long as the Garth was in commission.

September

In gratitude for the *Ocean Library*, which was sent by the pupils of the Holt School to the crew of HMS *Garth*, the pupils were sent by the crew a

1944 - 1944

beautiful model of the ship, made by some of the ship's company. The model still stands in the school library.

Model of HMS *Garth*

December

The Mayor was presented with a chess set made almost entirely of paper by scholars of St. Paul's School, when he attended the school breaking-up party to present prizes to the older children.

December 3rd

For the first time since the war the Wokingham Voluntary Fire Brigade resumed control of Wokingham Fire Station. From then it was manned part-time only.

December 18th

American troops arrived in Wokingham Evacuation Hospital (Semi-Mobile), Headquarters, UK. After a hot lunch at the bowling alley (now the Masons' Hall), members of the unit were assigned private billets. From there friendly contacts developed between the soldiers and the people of Wokingham.

1944

January

At a meeting of representatives of all organisations in the town it was agreed that the Americans should have the use of the large hall on Friday evenings. A committee was formed and Dr. E. F. Smith was elected secretary to provide entertainment for the troops.

1944 - 1944

March 3rd

Wokingham's British Welcome Club, created to bring the United States and Great Britain closer, was opened.

April

The Commander of HMS *Garth* appealed for five sets of Mah Jong. Six were donated.

April 28th

Wokingham's British Welcome Club was opened at the Town Hall. The object of these clubs, which opened over England, was to bring the U.S. and Great Britain closer together.

April 30th

The sight of two Italian prisoners of war strolling along Reading Road without an armed guard caused a resident to notify the police. As a precautionary measure the men, who could not speak a word of English, were interrogated and their camp was contacted. All was well and they were allowed to continue on their way.

June 5th

The avenues in and around Wokingham were lined with military vehicles in readiness for the invasion of Normandy.

June 6th

The Allied invasion of Normandy, *Operation Overlord,* the largest in history, commenced.

June 7th

Ald. William Thomas Martin and Dr. Ernest Ward, M.B.E. were made Honorary Freemen of the Borough of Wokingham.

Ald William. T. Martin J.P.
(1864-1951)

Dr. Ernest Ward M.B.E.
(1867-1957)

1944 - 1944

June 17th-23rd

Lieut. Col Edward J. C. King-Salter D.S.O. opened Wokingham District's "Salute the Soldier" week, The target was £350,000. A total of £489,903 was saved and Wokingham won the trophy which is now located outside the Town Hall Council Chamber.

October

The custom of ringing the curfew bell from September 18th to March 11th was revived in Wokingham. It had not been tolled since the beginning of hostilities.

October 11th

A pilot of an R.A.F. aircraft, Sqn Ldr. A, D. Miller, appeared before the East Berks. Coroner's Court at Wokingham to give evidence of the death of his technical observer, Mr. Peter Frank Ainsbury, a civilian technical officer attached to the Ministry of Aircraft Production who was killed when the machine crashed in flames near Woosehill Lane, Wokingham, on August 8th. The type of aircraft was not mentioned.

November

The presentation of the plaque to commemorate Wokingham's success in "Salute the Soldier" Week took place.

Salute the Soldier" plaque

1945 - 1945

December 3rd

Wokingham's 'D' Company 11th Berks. Home Guard stood down.

The last parade of Wokingham Home Guard

December 13th

A large party was held in Wokingham for children whose fathers were in the forces or Home Guard.

1945

January 26th

The schoolchildren of Wokingham and their parents gave a welcome to the officers and men of HMS *Garth* on their first official visit to the town. The crew also presented the district of Wokingham with a flag captured from a German E boat which HMS *Garth* had sunk.

The Mayor receives the German E-boat ensign
courtesy Wokingham Times

April 16th

Wokingham Town Council resolved to launch a fund for a '*Welcome Home for the Forces, 1945*'.

1945 - 1945

May 7th

Germany signed an unconditional surrender ending six years of war in Europe.

May 8th

The official declaration of Victory in Europe Day was celebrated in Wokingham with sober restraint. With a few exceptions, there were no scenes of wild enthusiasm, people generally, preferring to observe VE DAY in the privacy of their homes. To many whose husbands and sons were still fighting in the Far East, this was not their occasion for rejoicing. Flags, bunting and streamers were prolific, and displayed from almost every house in the district. More ambitious residents displayed fairy lights in their front gardens, while business premises and factories flood-lit their premises. Thanksgiving Services were held throughout the day in churches of all denominations. The services culminated in a United Thanksgiving Service held in the Market Place. At the conclusion everyone remained to listen to the broadcast of the King's speech. Afterwards they danced to the sounds of relayed music.

June 2nd

About fifty evacuee children and their foster mothers sat down to a farewell tea party at the Town Hall. The Mayor and Mayoress and other members of the Council were also present. After tea which included a large victory cake the children and grown-ups were entertained by the All Saints' Youth Club.

June 20th

Forty accompanied children and eleven adults and children from Wokingham Borough and Rural District returned to London. Before walking to the station they were given refreshments in St. Paul's Parish Rooms.

June 30th

Mrs. Jean Baxter, who had been the Hon. Secretary of Wokingham National Savings Committee for four years, resigned her appointment. During her term of office she has been responsible for the three successful savings campaigns - Warship Week, Wings for Victory and Salute the Soldier - which together totalled £1½ million in savings. Because of Mrs. Baxter's tireless efforts, savings in the district had risen from 17% to 32%.

1945 - 1945

Since the end of the war in Europe, they had fallen and Mrs. Baxter felt that she could no longer devote the time for this work.

August 15th

Wokingham celebrated V. J. Day (Victory in Japan Day) with a two-day holiday. Despite the heavy rain flags, bunting and streamers appeared. The churches held thanksgiving services and in the evening the Mayor and members of the Council attended a united service in All Saints Church. People danced in the Market Place until after midnight while in Peach Street shops were fully illuminated and lights stretched across the street. In Seaford Road a bonfire with an effigy on top of Hideki Tojo, war-time Prime Minster of Japan, was lit while children cheered.

September

Wokingham applied for a government loan for sodium street lighting.

September 28th

Holme Grange Preparatory School for Boys in Heathlands Road, Wokingham, was formally opened.

October

The Times and Weekly News opened new offices in Emmbrook.

The Times and Weekly News Emmbrook offices

December

The Government was accused of dragging its heels over Wokingham's house building programme while 400 applicants waited.

December 29th

The Hon. Mrs. Corfield and Miss Corfield were involved in a serious car accident on Saturday on their way to Edinburgh from Berwick. Mrs. Corfield was admitted to hospital suffering from severe cuts on her head, and shock. Miss Corfield escaped with bruises and minor cuts.

1946 - 1946

1946

The Malt House in Reading Road was sold to the Freemasons and became Downshire Lodge.

The Malt House © Jim Bell

Barnardo's Home for girls and small children opened in High Close.

January 1st

Peals of eight were rung at midnight from All Saints' and St. Paul's. Churches. A dance organised by the Wokingham branch of the Berkshire Regiment Old Comrades' Association was held in the Drill Hall.

February 4th

The first annual meeting of Wokingham Cricket Club since 1941 was held at the Club. Cllr. L. D. Sears, elected to the chair, said that he was keen to see cricket in Wokingham back to the standard he remembered some years ago. He stressed the need for enthusiasm and co-operation.

March

Flight Lieutenant A.F. Betts, whose wife and family lived at Toutley Hall, Wokingham, was mentioned in dispatches in the New Year's Honours List having, carried out special work in Italy. Flight Lieutenant Betts was still serving in the Central Mediterranean Forces and was officer in command of a parachute unit.

March

Mr. and Mrs. W. Smith, of *Holmwood*, Forest Road, Wokingham, were among the relatives who attended the memorial service at Colchester in remembrance of the officers and ship's company of the submarine HMS

1946 - 1946

Porpoise, which was presumed lost with all hands off the straits of Malacca in 1945. Their son, Roy, had been a member of the crew.

May 31st

Over 2,000 Dutch troops paraded before the Mayor and Members of the Wokingham Corporation before leaving for the Dutch East Indies.

Dutch troops paraded before the Mayor
Courtesy Wokingham Times

June

Cllr. Stanley L. Bowyer was mentioned in dispatches in recognition of his outstanding service with the B.L.A. (British Liberation Army) in Germany between the early part of 1944 and May 31st, 1945, when he was wounded. An acting sergeant, Cllr. Bowyer was with the allied Mission Camp, Main H.Q., 21st Army Group B.L.A.

June

For the first time in the history of the Borough, Wokingham would have a full-time Town Clerk at a salary of £500 per annum. He was Mr. Leonard G. Smalley, who was selected for the post from twenty-four applicants. Mr. Smalley succeeded Mr. J.H. Elliston Clifton, who retired from his official position on August 1st to devote more time to his legal practice.

1946 - 1946

August 4th

The first presentation of *Welcome Home Wallets* took place at the *Ritz* Cinema. The Mayor, Councillor David Goddard, presented 205 wallets of brown pigskin, each embossed with the crest of the Borough and endorsed with the initials of the recipient across the corner.

The first presentation of wallets at the Ritz cinema

This wallet was awarded to historian Ken Goatley

Courtesy Wokingham Times

September

Wokingham Town Council took over the former Toutley Military Camp for families on the emergency list to prevent squatters from getting there first, About ten families who had been living in crowded or insanitary conditions were moved in towards the end of the week.

September 17th

Many people watched a demonstration by Russian horsemen, the Don Cossack Riders, at Norris Farm. The performance was floodlit and proceeds went towards the Wokingham Welcome Home Fund.

1946 - 1946

September 28th

Wokingham's first Agricultural show for eight years took place.

September 28th

The fourth anniversary of the formation of the Corps was celebrated at the R.E.M.E. establishment at Arborfield. In the morning the men at Hazebrouck Barracks were inspected by Major-General Sir Basil A. Hill, C.B., C.B.E., D.S.O., one of the Colonels Commandant of the Corps, who was deputising for the Corps chief, Major-General Sir Bertram Rowcroft, who was indisposed.

October 27th

The second presentation of *Welcome Home Wallets* took place at the *Ritz* Cinema. The audience was larger than was present at the Ritz on Sunday afternoon. Every seat was occupied and other spectators were forced to stand almost three deep in places.

October 31st

The first 40 prefabricated houses (prefabs) were delivered to Wokingham to be installed in Binfield Road. Two were assembled every day.

November

Wokingham Town Council formally accepted the report of the General Purposes Committee and agreed to accept Mr. William T. Martin's figure of £12,000 for the pool and equipment payable by 30 annual instalments of £400 with the option of paying off the balance outstanding at any time.

December

The Town Council announced Its intention to purchase Martin's Pools for £12,000 to be paid in 30 instalments of £400.

December 21st

The Rose Hotel was damaged by fire. A member of the staff noticed a smell of burning emanating from a cloakroom on the top floor at about 11 p.m. The door of the room had been left locked by a plumber who had been busy there during the day dealing with a burst water pipe.

December 25th

Christmas festivities in Wokingham did not seem to be restricted to any serious extent by rationing. Patients at Wokingham Emergency Hospital began the day with ham for breakfast. Chicken, pork and Christmas pudding appeared at lunch-time, and iced cake, fruit jellies and trifle were provided for tea.

1947

January 25th

Lt.-Col. A.H. Gardner, R.A., of Lowther Road, Wokingham, was awarded the American Medal of Freedom. Lt.-Col. Gardner was decorated by an American Army Colonel, and the official citation read as follows: "For exceptional meritorious conduct in the performance of outstanding services in Italy from the 11th September, 1944, to 8th May, 1945."

May

Some 222 residents in the area petitioned for a halt or station between Wokingham and Crowthorne at Nine Mile Ride. The petition was sent to the traffic manager of the Southern Railway.

May 24th

The Wokingham Corporation officially re-opened Martin's Pools on Whit Saturday with a display by Ilford Diving Club.

July

Wokingham Allotment Holders' Association was formed.

July 7th

Members of the Methodist Youth Club welcomed a party of German Youth Leaders to their meeting. The Germans, mostly women, were on a visit to this country to study youth movements here. After seeing a play, "Anti-Clockwise," performed by their hosts, they joined in a game of table tennis. The reception committee was headed by Mr. Shanks, club leader.

July 10th

At a meeting of the Town Council it was unanimously resolved that 'the loyal and ancient Borough of Wokingham' would send a message of congratulations and goodwill to H.R.H. Princess Elizabeth on her engagement.

July 26th

Princess Elizabeth made her first official visit to the Royal Merchant Navy School at Bearwood since the announcement of her engagement. She attended prize-giving on Saturday to distribute the prizes and to unveil

1948 - 1948

a tablet acknowledging a gift to the school of £72,100 from the Merchant Navy Fund of South Africa.

October

A small group of people formed a dramatic society called the Wokingham Players.

October 10th

Miss Margaret Lockwood, a favourite British film star, visited Glebelands, the Cinema Trades Rest Home at Wokingham. She was received by Mr. Reginald Bromhead, chairman and president of the Home, and Mrs. Winifred Marshall, the matron. After lunch, Miss Lockwood made a tour of the house and grounds, expressing delight at what she saw. She chatted with the patients, some of whom were old colleagues, and left after tea.

November 10th

Cllr. the Hon. Mrs. Mary Hay Corfield, O.B.E., was elected Mayor of Wokingham, and thus became the first woman to hold this office in the borough.

Cllr. the Hon. Mrs. Mary Hay Corfield O.B.E. (1871-1965)

1948

Wokingham and District Chamber of Trade was created under the chairmanship of Mr. Stephen Sale.

Intensive municipal housing schemes were planned for Mylne Square, Barrett Crescent, Waterloo Road, Commons Road and Corfield Green.

The Duke of Kent commenced his education at Ludgrove School.

The Union Workhouse, which had been transformed into an emergency hospital, became Wokingham Hospital.

1948 - 1948

March 8th

A new full-time branch office of the Reading Trustee Savings Bank was opened at 31, Peach Street, Wokingham. by Sir Kenneth Stewart K.B.E., J.P., the chairman of the Trustee Savings Bank Association.

March 13th

Public support of Wokingham's "Silver Lining" Campaign was not as widespread as the organisers had hoped, and the audiences at functions in connection with the week were comparatively small. The Silver Lining Campaign was designed to encourage regular saving week by week.

March 20th

The closing of Wokingham's "Silver Lining" Campaign, marked by a concert by the Sainsbury Singers in the Town Hall was, perhaps the most disappointing event in a week full of discouragements. An excellent performance by Reading vocalists was heard by an audience of hardly more than a dozen. No charge for admission was made.

March 24th

Members of Wokingham Produce Association, with the help of the County Council's Agricultural Education Department, staged an exhibition of produce at the Town Hall. The Produce Association's main exhibit was a stand loaded with seasonable stock, together with preserves bottled by members.

April 7th

Miss B. E. Caudwell, the Principal, purchased the White House, Finchampstead Road, Wokingham, formerly occupied by Mr. C. S. Schofield. The house had some 20 rooms several of which were spacious and ideal for adaptation as class rooms.

1948 - 1948

White House School
courtesy Bracknell News

June

A painting of Mrs. Henrietta Walter, wife of former High Steward of Wokingham Arthur Fraser Walter, was presented to the Borough of Wokingham by Mr. John Walter of Bearwood.

Henrietta Maria Walter (1849-1937)

1948 - 1948

June

The executive of Wokingham's Welcome Home Fund for the Forces decided, with the approval of the Rector, to erect a stand and case in All Saints' Parish Church. The case would contain a book in which the names of those who fell in the 1914-1918 and 1939-1945 wars would be inscribed. This memorial would be dedicated by the Bishop of Oxford at a service on October 24th. Admission would be by ticket only owing to the need to reserve seats for the relatives of the fallen.

July

Traffic approaching Wokingham from London and Crowthorne no longer had to pull up at night and examine signposts to get their bearings, after bollards were installed in the Market Place by the Council. The bollards clearly showed the way to London, Reading, Crowthorne and other towns, and were situated at the Denmark and Peach Street sides of the Town Hall.

July 14th

Miss Anona Winn, the stage and radio star, visited the British Sailors' Society garden fete at the Holt School, Wokingham, and received donations from pupils of the school. Miss Winn spoke of the work done by the Society during the war. "Wokingham branch," she said, "raised over £1,000 in the past five years and this money was spent providing our sailors in all parts of the world with some of the comforts of home."

October 2 th

The Bishop of Oxford, Dr. Kenneth Kirk, attended a memorial service at All Saints' Church, Wokingham, to dedicate a Roll of Honour to local men and one local woman who died in both world wars. The memorial comprises a stand and case containing a book in which the names would be inscribed in due course.

November 20th

Representatives of the British Legion, the churches and the police force were among the large gathering who attended the opening of Wokingham Ex-Service Men's Club by the Mayor (Cllr. the Hon. Mrs. Corfield). The Club, near the British Legion Hall in Station Road, had three newly-decorated rooms - a men's bar, a ladies' bar, and a spacious billiards room upstairs. The chairman was Cllr. William J. Willey.

1949 - 1949

December

Sir Richard and Lady White, and their twelve-years-old Boxer, "Boy," holder of the dogs' V.C., the Dickin Medal, visited Wokingham. "Boy," who had been trained to detect mines, accompanied the invasion forces which landed on the continent on "D" Day. As the result of a bullet wound he lost the sight of one eye. The Dickin Medal was awarded for his devotion.

1949

The Sale family donated a part of their orchard land near Cockpit Path to the town to accommodate *Sales Memorial Bungalows* in memory of Philip Sale (1861-1947), Mayor, Alderman and Freeman of the Borough.

January

Mr. Arthur Tyndale Heelas, of Oakleigh, Fairview Road, Wokingham, head of Heelas, Ltd., and an authority of the history of the town, left two pictures and his library of reference books, archaeological journals, and books dealing with local history, to the Mayor and Corporation of Wokingham, suggesting that the collection be used as a reference library and not as a loan library.

January 1st

The Wokingham Allotment Holders Association changed its name to Wokingham Allotments & Gardens Association.

January 6th

Residents and staff of Buzzacott Hall, the Salvation Army's Eventide Home at Wokingham, joined in a farewell luncheon in honour of their retiring warden, Colonel Evelyn Farey. Visitors included Mr. James Buzzacott, donor of the house, and the Rev. Gordon Kenworthy, Rector of All Saints', Wokingham.

May

Since the start of the Territorial Army recruiting campaign there had been no response in Wokingham to the appeals and the local strength still stood at five officers and five other ranks. In an effort to stimulate recruiting for the T.A. and the R.A.F. Voluntary Reserves, the 4/6th Battalion, the Royal Berkshire Regiment, T.A., held a parade and a series of displays in Wokingham.

1949 - 1949

May 8th

Wokingham and District Boy Scouts Association annual meeting was held in the Town Hall. The District Commissioner, Mr. R.B.J. Moffitt, reported a loss in membership of eight, largely due to the closing down of a Bearwood Troop. He said that the problem of obtaining Scout Leaders was becoming increasingly difficult.

June 8th

Wokingham celebrated Victory Day with a united service in the Market Place and other events.

July 14th

Sweets were again rationed from August 14th. This was one of several changes in the rationing scheme announced in the House of Commons by Sir Stafford Cripps, Chancellor of the Exchequer, when he opened the debate on the economic situation.

September 4th

Sodium street lights were switched on for the first time, replacing gas lighting.

Sodium lights Switched on September 1949

1950 - 1951

October 6th-12th

Wokingham celebrated *Thanksgiving Week* with concerts, dances and competitions.

December 27th

British film stars Anna Neagle and Joan Dowling sent Christmas presents and cigarettes for residents of Glebelands Convalescent Home. Wokingham. These and other presents were placed on a large Christmas tree and distributed to residents at a Christmas party.

1950

Wokingham became a parliamentary constituency and the first election was held for the new Wokingham Division. The Conservative candidate, the Hon. Peter Farquharson Remnant, won the seat.

The Wokingham Allotments & Gardens Association changed its name to Wokingham Allotment Holders & Gardeners Association.

June 2nd/3rd

Petrol rationing because of the Suez crisis ended from midnight. It was forecast that whatever time was saved in the garages by the abolition of coupons would be more than filled by the anticipated increase in repair work.

September 5th

Wokingham held its first post-war carnival with a non-stop variety programme of music, shows and sports culminating in a grand procession of nearly 100 decorated vehicles.

November 30th

After eleven years the Women's Land Army in Berkshire was disbanded. The Land Army formed an emergency labour force during both world wars upon which farmers learned to depend for the efficient working of their farms.

1951

Construction of a new school, St. Crispin's, on the London Road commenced. It was to be a model for the future.

1951 - 1951

January 6th

The *Savoy Cinema* closed down. The last film to be shown was *The Champion*.

March 9th

The Rotary Club of Wokingham was founded.

May

Members of Wokingham youth organisations celebrated the Festival of Britain by relaying a flaming torch lit by Ald. Frank S. Perkins at Shute End, to The Mayor Cllr. Stanley L. Bowyer, who used it to light Wokingham's Bonfire.

May 1st

The new library at Montague House was opened by the Mayor of Wokingham Cllr. Stanley L. Bowyer. The entrance to the library was on the right hand side of the building. The library until then had been in the Town Hall.

Montague House, Wokingham's new Library

May 16th

The Wokingham Rotary Club, with 26 members, received its Charter at Wokingham Town Hall which marked the end of its probationary period.

1951 - 1951

September 5th

The Mayor of Wokingham, Cllr. William J. Willey, opened Wokingham's Festival Carnival by releasing the first balloon of a balloon race in the Market Place. Then the carnival queen and her attendants arrived and were welcomed by several thousand spectators. After opening the fun-fair and touring the attractions she proceeded to the Carnival Field where she declared it open for the children's races and other events. The climax of the day was the procession which stretched for nearly two miles. Included were tableaux, decorated vehicles, motor-cycles, bicycles, and hansom-cabs. A variety concert took place in the Market Place and dancing continued until the following morning to music by the R.E.M.E. orchestra in the Drill Hall.

September 29th

The R.E.M.E. celebrated its ninth anniversary at Arborfield Garrison.

October 1st

News reached Wokingham that two soldiers, Privates Arthur Allum and Edward Rose, believed to have been killed in the Korean War, were still alive.

November 14th

Wokingham opened its first Industries Exhibition.

December 8th

The 500th anniversary of the John Westende Charity was celebrated at the almshouses in Peach Street. The charity had provided funds for the construction of thirteen almshouses.

1952 - 1952

December 12th

A fire severely damaged the Metalair Factory in Station Road.

1952

February 7th

King George VI died at Sandringham House and his elder daughter, Elizabeth Alexandra Mary Windsor became Queen Elizabeth II, Queen of the United Kingdom and the other Commonwealth realms.

February 9th

The Mayor Cllr William Willey read the Proclamation of the Accession of Queen Elizabeth II to the throne.

April 23rd

Margaret Isabel Ellison, the last member of the Ellison family of *The Elms House,* died. She left Elms Field to the people of Wokingham.

August 27th

Thousands of people came to Wokingham Carnival from neighbouring towns and villages. The Mayor of Wokingham, Cllr. A.T. Ilott, officially opened Carnival Day by releasing the first of many balloons from the Market Place. The Carnival Queen was crowned by the Mayoress. The Dagenham Girl Pipers paraded and later returned to accompany a display of highland dancing. At Wokingham Hospital, the Queen visited patients including Mr. Beesley, aged 105, who received a kiss from her Majesty. Late afternoon there was a grand parade of cars of vintage and 1952 models. The borough dust cart received coins for the Lynmouth Disaster Fund. Profits from the Carnival also went towards the Fund.

The Dagenham Girl Pipers

1953 - 1953

October

Consent was given by the Minister of Transport to install a skeleton lighting scheme in Molly Millars Lane and Eastheath Avenue planned by Wokingham Borough Council.

1953

On its 50th anniversary the *Wokingham and Bracknell Times* returned to Peach Street.

April 14th

St. Crispin's School was opened unofficially with 230 pupils.

St. Crispin's Secondary Modern School

June 2nd to 7th

Wokingham celebrated the Coronation of Elizabeth II. As part of the celebrations an ox was roasted in the Market Place. The week of festivities officially began on Monday evening with a united church service in the Market Place. On Tuesday the old folks' tea was held in the Waterloo Restaurant, followed by a concert. The Coronation Ball was held in the Drill Hall. The children were catered for and their big day was Wednesday. Some 150 entrants in fancy dress marched down Denmark Street to Langborough Road Recreation Ground where they paraded. They then went into the marquees for the Coronation tea party and each was given a souvenir mug. After tea they enjoyed sports and a puppet show. Dancers from the Drill Hall and Waterloo Restaurant came to watch the Mayor of

1953 - 1953

Wokingham, Cllr. Walter G. Jackson, light the fire. Cooking of the ox began at 2 am on Saturday and was completed at mid-day. By 4 o'clock the Market Place was filled with over 1,500 people. The Mayor carved the first portion then nearly 2,000 pieces were served to the public, most of whom purchased a slice of bread and a picnic plate for threepence.

The ox roast in the Market Place
courtesy Wokingham Times

September 16th
Privates Arthur John Allum and Edward Sidney Rose returned to Wokingham after spending two and a half years in a Korean prisoner-of-war camp.

October 8th
The Mayor of Wokingham, Cllr. Walter G. Jackson, made presentations to the two soldiers at a Town Council meeting in Wokingham Town Hall.

October 14th
The Minister of Education, Miss Florence Horsbrugh, officially opened the Wokingham Secondary Modern School (St. Crispin's) and planted a tree.

1954 - 1954

November

The Town Clerk, Mr. L. G. Smalley, received the coat of arms granted to the Wokingham Borough from the Royal College of Arms under the Letters Patent by the Kings of Arms.

Wokingham Coat of Arms

November

London County Council and Wokingham Borough Council met to discuss the possibility of housing 5,000 of London's population.

November 1st

The Wokingham Produce Association merged with the Wokingham Allotment Holders & Gardeners Association to form the Wokingham Horticultural Association.

November 13th

Princess Margaret visited Dr. Bernardo's Homes to open the first of three new cottage homes.

1954

February

Wokingham received its new lever press seal-embossing machine which did away with having to melt and use sealing wax.

June 12th

The Ex-service Men's Club closed because of a reduction of support by its members.

June 14th

Most of Heathlands Estate, the former home of Mrs. W. Howard Palmer, was sold by auction.

1955 - 1955

August 21st

The Wokingham Horticultural Association held its first show and gymkhana at Frog Hall Meadow.

1955

Wokingham was divided into the electoral wards of Norreys, Evendons, Emmbrook, West, Wescott and Langborough. Three councillors were allocated to each ward.

March 2nd

Wokingham Borough Council rejected a proposal to accept 5,000 Londoners to Wokingham.

March 8th

It was decided not to hold a carnival that year because the profit from the previous year's carnival was slightly less than 10% of the total income.

April 22nd

Well-known child film star, 10 year-old Miss Mandy Miller, paid a visit to Glebelands, the Cinematograph Trades Benevolent Fund country home, and presented a "deep freeze" refrigerator to the matron.

September

William Chambers donated a print of an ancestor, Thomas Chambers, mace bearer, town crier and sexton of the town from 1826 to 1861, to Wokingham Town Hall.

Thomas Chambers (1797-1861)

1956 - 1956

December

The Wokingham Patriotic Fund, set up in October, 1899 by Captain Arthur Hill, 6th Marquess of Downshire, M.P., for the benefit of widows and orphans for the South African War, was closed without one claim having been made upon it.

1956

Norreys Hall Evangelical Church was built in Norreys Avenue. The Open Brethren had held meetings in Wokingham since 1940 but this was their first permanent place of assembly.

Wokingham Borough Council purchased Elms Field from the Ellison estate for £8,900 for use as a 'public open space'.

January 1st

The 1st and 5th Wokingham Scout groups amalgamated to form a new group, the 3rd Wokingham.

March

The former N.A.A.F.I. hut on the Toutley Military Camp was sold by the Town Council for £22 10s.

June 6

Wescott Road School celebrated its golden jubilee.

June 27th

A fire seriously damaged the upper floor of Heelas departmental store.

1957 - 1958

1957

February

The Wokingham Colour Photo Society was founded.

May

Several sixth-formers from Wokingham County Girls' School were seen in Wokingham wearing their new summer headwear of straw boaters with red and white bands.

1958

Sir William Radcliffe van Straubenzie was elected M.P. for Wokingham.

Sir William Radcliffe van Straubenzie (1924-1999)

January

Mr. W. W. Stewart, who had carried on a cycle trade at the corner of Rose Street and the Market Place for the past 21 years, closed his shop for the last time.

February 14th

An unexploded German bomb from the Second World War was found in the garden of an unoccupied house behind Peach Street.

March 13th

Mr. John Walter V presented a silver-gilt cup to the Mayor of Wokingham. The cup was originally presented by the residents of Bearwood to Mr. and Mrs. Arthur F. Walter in October 1897.

John Walter V (1873-1969)

Cup presented by John Walter

131

1959 - 1959

May 26th

The Wokingham sub-branch of the Garth Hunt branch of the Pony Club and the local St. John Ambulance Brigade joined forces to stage the first Wokingham Pony Show and Gymkhana, held on the Carnival Field.

September

A set of brass measures made in 1857 was donated to Wokingham by the Weights and Measures Department of the County Council. This set of ten measures was originally issued to the police of Wokingham, who were then responsible for the enforcement of the newly-introduced Act of 1855 governing the uniformity of weights and measures.

September 6th

Moses Dance, caretaker of Wokingham Town Hall, worked from 6.00 until 8.00 am then went home for his usual cup of tea. Upon his return an hour later he began to clean the Council Chamber and had just swept some dust through the door to the landing when part of the Chamber ceiling made of heavy plaster fell where he had been standing a few seconds previously.

October

Cllr. Dorothy Wescott donated to Wokingham Town Hall the illuminated address presented to her father Mr. Thomas Manley Wescott, first Mayor of Wokingham, on completion of his two-year term of office.

October 9th

Wokingham Town Council conferred upon Ald. Ernest. W. Reeves the freedom of the borough in recognition of the faithful and devoted service which he had rendered to the borough of Wokingham and to the County of Berkshire by his long association with local government over the previous thirty-five years, and his interest in the social, recreational and cultural life of the town.

November

It was reported that The Wokingham Ex-Service Men's Club was likely to be closed down.

1959

Oakfield School founded in 1895 and Luckley School founded in 1918 merged.

1959 - 1959

February 18th

At a poorly attended meeting in Wokingham Town Hall it was decided not to have a carnival that year.

February 19th

At a ceremony Ald. Ernest William Reeves (1890-1963) was made Honorary Freedman of the Borough of Wokingham in recognition of the faithful and devoted service which he had rendered to the borough of Wokingham and to the County of Berkshire by his long association with local government over the previous thirty-five years, and his interest in the social, recreational and cultural life of the town.

Ald Ernest William Reeves (1890-1963)

June 22nd

The factory of Ladybird Appliances Ltd. in Oxford Road was destroyed by fire.

August

The Wokingham Players were given permission to erect a theatre on a site on Norreys Barn Estate. The *theatre* comprised two wooden army huts that the Players had purchased for £100. The chosen site for the theatre was where Stephanie Chase Court now stands.

August

Workmen starting on the last phase of the restoration of All Saints' Church discovered a lead coffin in a cavity under the chancel when the chancel was being redecorated. The cavity was thought to have been caused by a defective drainage system. The graves, which had been revealed by the subsidence, were thought to be 250 years old.

August 25th

Fred Painter, blacksmith of 43, Peach Street, Wokingham, was presented with a portrait of himself to commemorate 53 years of service at his smithy.

1959 - 1959

Fred Painter
(1883-1969)

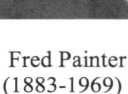

Fred's Smithy in Peach Street

The Public Buildings and Properties Committee of the Town Council reported that the Roll of Honour had been seriously affected by dampness, and could not be re-erected in the Town Hall without considerable renovation and re-writing of the names. The Committee discussed the suitability or otherwise of using the Town Hall annexe for the Roll of Honour and suggested that it could be hung in the memorial clinic in Denmark Street. Some Town councillors strongly disagreed with this and also condemned the lack of respect shown to the Roll of Honour by townspeople who had hung coats and put cups of tea on it at the previous meeting of the Town Council.

September

Work to renovate two Queen Victoria almshouses in Peach Street was completed.

November

Premium bonds were sold in Wokingham which was the first town to sell them.

November 28th

The Wokingham Plastics Factory in Denton Road was almost destroyed by fire.

1960 - 1960

December 11th

James Butler 6th Marquess of Ormonde, C.V.O., M.C. was appointed 17th High Steward of Wokingham.

James Butler, 6th Marquess of Ormonde, (1893-1971)

1960

February

During December ten cases of scarlet fever and two cases of pulmonary tuberculosis, one man and one woman, had been notified to the Medical Officer of Health for Wokingham. There were now 40 men and 35 women in the town suffering from this form of tuberculosis.

February 10th

The Howard Palmer Bowling Club was separated from the Wokingham Club which was virtually bankrupt.

February 10th

It was resolved at a Town Council meeting that the century-old Town Hall mirror should be repaired at a cost of £50 and re-hung in its original position in Wokingham Town Hall.

March 22nd

At a special meeting of the Wokingham Club members decided to continue the Howard Palmer Bowling Club.

May 23rd

The Hon. Peter Remnant, M.P. for the Wokingham Division for nine years, retired.

30th July

The Wokingham Club was closed by its President Reginald H. R. Palmer because of declining membership.

1961 - 1961

July

Wokingham Borough Council announced a competition for the best design of a new Town Hall and municipal offices. The first prize was £1,000 and the site would be at the junction of Wellington Road and Denmark Street.

July

The Baptist chapel in Milton Road was considered to be inadequate and work to build a larger one commenced.

October

It was resolved that the Roll of Honour commemorating those Wokingham men who had died during the 1914-18 and 1939-45 wars, would be restored in time for the annual service of remembrance and wreath-laying ceremony. The restored Roll of Honour would not be glass covered, as it was being written on oak panelling. The annexe, in which the Roll would remain, despite a suggestion some months previously that it should be moved to the Denmark Street Clinic, had been used as a workroom by the artist employed by the Council to restore old Town Hall paintings. The work had since been completed and therefore the annexe would no longer be required for that purpose.

November 3rd

The winning design for Wokingham's new Town Hall and municipal offices was submitted by John G. Fryman, of Marlow.

December 8th

At a council meeting a demand was made for more information to be obtained regarding the costs of building the proposed new Town Hall and municipal buildings for Wokingham.

1961

Provisional plans for an Inner Distribution Road (I.D.R.) were drawn up.

January 19th

Wokingham Hospital maternity unit was opened by Sir George Schuster, chairman of the Oxford Regional Hospital Board.

1961 - 1961

February 26th

Girl Guides attended the evening service at All Saints' Church for the blessing of two new banners of the Wokingham 4th and 5th companies.

April

The Caiger sisters refused to vacate their closed 100-year-old family shoe business at No. 13 Peach Street.

Caiger, Footwear Retailer
courtesy Goatley Collection

April

The Welcome Inn in Peach Street was sold by Brakespeare's and was demolished to make way for a block of shops.

The Welcome Inn
courtesy Wokingham Convent

April 29th

Mr. and Mrs. Alfred Tompkins of the confectioners at the corner of Rose Street and Broad Street retired and the building was to be demolished at a later date to enable the entrance to Rose Street to be widened.

137

1961 - 1961

June 16th

Bèches Manor Hotel was completely destroyed by fire. The building was empty and scheduled for preservation because of historical and architectural interest.

Bèches Manor Hotel

July 8th

The Mayor of Wokingham, Cllr. Dr. Phyllys Pigott, officially opened the C. M. Woolf Memorial Cottages at *Glebelands*, the Cinematograph Trade Benevolent Fund's home.

1961 - 1961

September 16th

Percy Chapman, the Berkshire County cricketer, who became captain of England and one of the great personalities of the game, died in an Alton hospital aged 61. Born in Reading in September 1900, he was the son of Mr. Frank Emerson Chapman of Wokingham, former Wokingham Town Councillor who lived in Wiltshire Road. Percy was buried in All Saints' Churchyard, Wokingham.

Arthur Percy Frank Chapman (1900-1961)

November 9th

The Mayor of Wokingham, Cllr. Dr. Phyllys P. Pigott, presented Cyril Nibbs, Mace-Bearer, with a 70th birthday present of money in honour of his twenty-two years' service.

Cyril Alfred Nibbs, Macebearer (1893-1981)

139

1962 - 1962

December 4th

The first supermarket in Wokingham, Fine Fare, opened at No.74 Peach Street and started a price-reduction war. The first 150 customers received a free chicken and over the following days Fine Fare gave 7,000 frozen birds to early morning customers or to those purchasing £2 worth or more of goods.

December 26th

The Garth Hunt held its final meet in the Market Place.

Garth Hunt meet in the Market Place
Courtesy Arborfield Local History Society

1962

St. Paul's School at Shute End became the Walter County Infants School.

Bernie Inns purchased The Rose Inn.

Poet John Betjeman presented prizes at Holt School.

January

During the first week in January bulldozers from town building and demolition sites were hired out, and a number of snow ploughs patrolled the town centre shovelling and scraping the snow off the roads. Gangs of workmen also cleared paths caked with ice and snow.

January

The engagement was announced of Mr. Alan Godsal of Haines Hill, Twyford, and Lady Elizabeth Stopford, younger daughter of the 8th Earl of Courtown, of Beaconsfield, and Mrs. Christopher Vian, of Godalming.

1962 - 1962

January

A seven feet long Christmas cracker containing 84 pounds of chocolates was given to the children of Dr. Barnardo's Home, High Close, Wokingham, by the *tin-bashers* of Handley Page, Woodley. The cracker that was delivered on the Saturday before Christmas was to stay unopened until the children returned.

June 11th

The *Royal Exchange* public house in Denmark Street, Wokingham, closed on Whit-Monday evening to make way for development.

The Royal 'Exchange

June 25th

H. M. The Queen and the Duke of Edinburgh visited Wokingham. A gaily-decorated Wokingham, hung with flags and bunting, welcomed the Queen and the Duke of Edinburgh on their arrival in the afternoon. Her Majesty signed the Distinguished Visitors' Book and her photograph now hangs in the Council Chamber.

1962 - 1962

June 30th

The Carnival programme opened with an amateur contest at the Ritz cinema on Carnival eve, but the official start to the day was the opening ceremony by the Mayor, Dr. P.P. Pigott, in Rose Street car park. The Carnival Queen arrived at Langborough Playing Field in an open landau drawn by two greys and was crowned by the Mayoress, Mrs. H. I. Cozens. The feature of the day was the procession. Quite outstanding was a float depicting a pink elephant that waved its ears and trumpeted realistically. A formal carnival ball was held at the Drill Hall and a "twisting" one in the open air on the recreation ground. Then, as night fell, people flocked to see a firework display.

July

Outline plans for the first stage of the municipal offices at Wellington Road were approved by the Berkshire County Planning Committee.

September 29th

A ceremony was held to mark the completion of the 750th permanent post-war council house dwelling at the Norreys Barn Estate.

October 11th

The walnut tree around which a seat in memory of the late Ald. Philip Sale was built between the Sale Memorial Homes and the Waterloo Restaurant, was felled as the top had died and was brittle.

The Walnut tree with members of the Sale family sitting on "Philip's Seat"

1963 - 1963

November

A new coat-of-arms was granted to Wokingham Rural District Council. The design combined the principal topographical and historical features of the district, and the motto Unum E pluribus (*One made out of many*) referred to the union of the various parishes in one rural district. It was a variant of the motto of the United States of America, whose first president, George Washington, was descended in the maternal line from the family of Ball of Arborfield.

November 22nd

The Tudor-styled building opposite the Town Hall that had been the home of Sale and Son (Wokingham), Ltd. since 1892 was sold for £23,000 to Messrs. J. Kirby & Co., of Molly Millars Lane, Wokingham.

Sale & Son Ltd building opposite the Town Hall

December

Fog blanketed Wokingham for five days.

1963

Goatley Printing Works moved from the Market Place to Norton Road.

1963 - 1963

Anthony Cross founded The Wokingham Society.

January 3rd

Trains carrying hundreds of passengers to work were stranded between Ascot and Wokingham yesterday morning as ice brought electric trains to a complete standstill.

March 8th

Norreys Barn Theatre was officially opened by the Mayor, Cllr. Dr. Phyllys. P. Pigott.

Norreys Barn Theatre
courtesy Wokingham Times

June

Officials from British Railways attending a public meeting in Wokingham were the target for a storm of protests about the new level-crossing barriers because they often did not function.

June 3rd

Princess Anne was one of the entrants at Wokingham Pony Show and Gymkhana held at the Elms Field on Whit-Monday. She won the trophy for the best rider under 13.

July

Wokingham Town Council's detailed plans for the first stage of the scheme for their new municipal offices on The Elms open space at Wellington Road, Wokingham were approved by the Berkshire County Planning Committee. The scheme comprised a modern styled three-storey office block with a flat roof and a finish of blue-brown brindled facing bricks with black vitrolite panels and courses of tooled precast concrete.

July 11th

A week after they were officially brought into use the automatic barriers at the Star Lane level crossing failed twice. The fault lay in a manufacturing defect in a piece of electrical equipment.

1964 - 1964

October

At the annual meeting of the Parent Teacher Association it was reported that since Easter at St. Paul's School, Wokingham, three new Terrapin buildings had been erected in the playing field, and the school interior had been repainted in attractive colours. The Infant and Junior Schools had been amalgamated under one head, and new staff had been engaged to cope with the increasing number of children.

October

After having been for sale for three years, the former Wokingham Club premises were sold. Mr. Colin Farnell, sole principal of Messrs. H. E. Hall and Son, confirmed that the freehold of the property, owned by Mr. Reginald H. R. Palmer, had been sold to a London property investment company. The undisclosed price was understood to be substantial and ran into five figures.

November 5th

At a meeting of Wokingham Town Council's General Purpose Committee it was said that work on the first stage of the new Wokingham municipal buildings and public hall was expected to start by April 1964. At the meeting was the architect, Mr. John Fryman, who in 1960 won £1,000 in a competition to design the new buildings. He explained that, soon after the competition, there was a national financial crisis and local government capital expenditure was heavily curtailed, resulting in a reduced and less expensive building plan.

Some time later the Town Council decided not to move from its existing Town Hall premises and the new building would therefore be occupied solely by the Borough Council.

1964

Palmer School became a controlled school when the managers relinquished its Aided Status.

March

Professor Sir Colin Buchanan, town planner, declared that Wokingham needed a bypass.

1964 - 1964

May 23rd

The foundation stone of the modified Wesleyan Church Centre in Rose Street was laid.

September 6th

After alterations to the building in Easthampstead Road had been completed the Catholic school opened as St. Theresa's R. C. (Aided) Primary School.

December

The old mill and the mill house at Emmbrook were demolished to make way for a petrol station.

The old mill and the mill house at Emmbrook

December 5th

The new Methodist Church Hall and ancillary buildings in Rose Street were opened by Mrs. A. H. Creed.

Methodist Church Rooms
courtesy Methodist Church

1965

Plans were passed for the redevelopment of Peach Street and Market Place which involved the demolition of a number of properties.

The Waterloo Restaurant, formerly the British Restaurant, in Cockpit Path was demolished.

Wokingham Council Offices in Wellington Road were formally opened.

Wokingham Council Offices

January 30th

The Wokingham public saw Sir Winston Churchill's funeral train from a goods siding as it travelled to Bladon. Churches were filled on Sunday for memorial services.

February

The Wokingham Society published their views on the Berkshire County Council proposals for the redevelopment of the town centre.

April 20th

The official opening of South-East and Central Berkshire's first Youth Week in Wokingham was launched from St. Crispin's School where a three-day programme of events was staged.

May 3rd

Emmbrook School was opened as a two-form entry County Secondary School. Emmbrook Junior School, formerly Emmbrook County Secondary, and Emmbrook Infant School were officially opened.

July 16th

The automatic barriers at the Star Lane level crossing, Wokingham, failed in the "open" position for road traffic. They were out of action for five hours.

1966 - 1967

October

The 400-strong Wokingham Society set out to plot stage by stage the growth of the town as its members imagined it in the years to come.

1966

The demolition of Peach Street premises between Nos. 28 and Nos. 32, and Market Place premises Nos. 20 and 21 commenced.

January 21st

Heelas Department Store in the Market Place was closed to make way for the Boots complex.

Heelas of Wokingham Ltd. (c1798-1966)   Goatley Collection

July 16th

Cecil Nibbs, the oldest mace-bearer in Britain, was presented with a tankard when he retired from office at Wokingham Town Hall. His work as mace-bearer spanned 26 years of mayoralty.

September

The first, second and third year pupils of St. Paul's Primary School moved into one wing of their new school in Murray Road.

1967

The development of the old Heelas store site commenced.

1967 - 1967

A debate took place about whether to retain the Overhangs on Peach Street or replace them with shops.

The Overhangs

The old *Royal Exchange* public-house in Denmark Street was demolished.

January 10th

At the annual meeting of the Wokingham and District Agriculture Association it was announced that the Wokingham Show would return to Wokingham that year after an absence of several years. It was to be held at Woods Farm, Easthampstead Road, Wokingham.

February

At a meeting, attended by only six members, it was decided to close the Howard Palmer Bowling Club. Although the Club had found itself in the position of having a good green and two useful pavilions, it did not have a strong following of members.

April

Berkshire police were granted permission by Wokingham Borough Council to use the Carnival Field in Wellington Road as a landing area for helicopters. Helicopters were used by the police to combat crime and pinpoint traffic hold-ups.

1968 - 1968

April 13th

At a meeting in Wokingham Town Hall officers of the 4/6th Battalion of the Royal Berkshire Regiment, which had been disbanded in February, presented a silver cup (the Sandhurst Cup) to the Mayor, Cllr. William C. A. Smith, which had been given to the Regiment in 1868.

Sandhurst Cup
Courtesy Wokingham Town Council

September

At a Town Council meeting confirmation was received from Reginald Palmer's solicitors stating that Mr. Palmer was prepared to make a gift of the bowling green to the corporation provided that the corporation would enter into a covenant to use the land for public recreation purposes and designate the land as Howard Palmer Recreation Ground.

1968

The former Wokingham Club bowling green was given to Wokingham Town Council by Deed of Gift to perpetuate the memory of Howard Palmer.

Waitrose Supermarket was formally opened in Peach Street.

The Overhangs were purchased by a Wokingham builder who hoped to transform them into a commercial proposition by the end of the year.

March

Two Bailey bridges were installed to take traffic to enable work to widen Skew Bridge in Reading Road.

September 6th

The first evening of Bingo at the Ritz in Finchampstead Road took place.

September 16th

There was chaos after 40 hours of continuous rain flooded parts of Barkham Road, Wokingham, and Ascot. Between 9.00 a.m. on Sunday and 9.00 a.m. on Monday 2.5 inches of rain fell.

1969 - 1969

September 29th

Wokingham's experimental one-way traffic scheme came into operation at midnight on Sunday, September 29th. The Borough Engineer issued a warning to motorists that workmen would be on the roads all day and possibly on the following Monday erecting new islands and signage.

October

The new one-way experimental traffic scheme raised a storm of protest from householders in Langborough Road, Murdoch Road, Crescent Road and Howard Road. The result was described as becoming like Piccadilly Circus.

2nd December

Mayor Cllr. Jean Davy launched an appeal for £50,000-£60,000 to equip a day centre for the newly-formed Wokingham & District Old People's Welfare Centre, later known as W.A.D.E.

Jean Marjorie Davy (1915-1987)

December

Work began to demolish the bakehouse and garage premises in Rose Street at the junction with Broad Street to provide a wider access to Rose Street.

1969

The fire station moved from Wokingham Town Hall to the site of the Plastics Factory in Denton Road.

Public meetings took place in Wokingham Town Hall to debate a proposed £13 million A329 link road.

January 25th

The Wokingham Society held an exhibition in Wokingham Town Hall to increase public interest in the future development in the town and in the town's past.

1970 - 1970

February 6th

The first Meals-on-Wheels in Wokingham were delivered by Mayor Cllr. Jean Davey.

February 16th

Franklin Engelmann of the BBC radio programme *Down Your Way* visited Wokingham.

September 12th

The M4 route was given the go-ahead and a compulsory order was issued for land for the Theale to Winnersh section.

November

The junior section of St. Paul's School moved to a new site in Murray Road and became the State Aided St. Paul's Church of England Junior School. The Infant Section became controlled and remained in the original buildings as Walter County Infants School.

November

3,000 Wokingham households petitioned against the A329 Reading-Wokingham relief road.

1970

The former Tudor George Inn on the corner of Rose Street, then a bakery, was demolished and replaced some years later by an extension to the National Westminster Bank

Sir William van Straubenzee, Wokingham MP for nearly twenty-eight years, retired.

Keephatch Primary School, Ashridge Road, was opened.

1970 - 1970

January

Wokingham Laundry of Station Road was acquired by Maidenhead District Laundry Co. Ltd.

May

A hoard of Roman coins of the 4th century A.D. was discovered in an Emmbrook field by a woman walking her dog.

September 11th

The Youth Centre in Broad Street, founded by Cllr. John West, was officially opened.

October

Palmer Court old people's flats were officially opened by the Mayor of Wokingham, Cllr. John West.

November 14th

The new Corpus Christi Roman Catholic Church in Sturges Road was consecrated by Derek Worlock, Bishop of Portsmouth, and Corpus Christie Church in the Terrace was closed.

The new Corpus Christi Roman Catholic Church © Jim Bell

November 20th

Part of the former Fire Station at Wokingham Town Hall was opened as a W.A.D.E. (Wokingham and District Association for the Elderly) charity shop.

November 22nd

The Mayor of Wokingham, Cllr. John West, while strolling in the Market Place was told to move on by a crew making a film starring Mia Farrow.

1971 - 1971

1971

Plans for an inner distribution road (I.D.R.) around Wokingham were put forward.

January

It was decided to demolish Market House, former meeting place of the Wokingham Club, because of its dangerous condition.

January 7th

The results of a structural survey of the blacksmith's shop in Peach Street were submitted at a meeting at Wokingham Public Works Committee. The Committee was looking into uses for the premises which were to be preserved.

April

All Saints Church launched an appeal for £46,000 to fund a modern parish centre.

April 23rd

The Wokingham Laundry Co. Ltd. in Station Road was closed down and the work was transferred to Hobbs West Reading Linen Service. The site was disposed of for residential purposes.

April 17th

James Butler, 6th Marquess of Ormonde, C.V.O., M.C. 17th High Steward of Wokingham, died.

May 13th

The Rose Inn was severely damaged by fire to an estimated sum of £100,000. Wokingham's Chamber of Trade called for a full-time fire brigade.

June

Wokingham Borough Council's Parks Committee decided to open the former Howard Palmer Bowling Green for recreation purposes.

July

Work to widen the Skew Bridge on the Reading Road was completed. The work took almost four years to complete.

1972 - 1972

August

A block of Almshouses at the junction of Peach and Cross Streets was demolished by the Charity Commissioners as part of the proposed re-development for the area.

The demolished almshouses
Goatley Collection

October
Wokingham Council decided to develop Woosehill.

1972
After many trials, Wokingham's one-way system was adopted.

The Wokingham Society called for a public inquiry into the Woosehill development.

January 27th
The controversial Blue Pool near Blagrove Lane was discussed at a Town Council meeting with regard to the nuisance and dangers and smell of mud in that area caused by vehicles travelling to and from the Pool.

April
Fairview Estates Ltd. purchased 25.40 acres of land at Woosehill for residential development.

May 30th
Circuses would be allowed to continue using the Wokingham Carnival Field provided an R.S.P.C.A. Inspector could visit the site at any time.

The northern by-pass was opened following the completion of the final section of the A329(M) from the Wokingham-Twyford Road to Amen Corner.

1973 - 1973

1973

January

A six-week inquiry was held into an application to develop 325 acres of land at Woosehill to provide housing for about 7,000 people, thus increasing the population of the town by one third. Despite almost unanimous local opposition the application was granted.

January 21st

Over 600 people walked 20 miles in aid of WADE. Sponsorship of over £4,000 had been promised.

January 30th

At a ceremony Ald. Stanley Leonard Bowyer and Town Clerk Leonard Goddard Smalley were made Honorary Freemen of the Borough of Wokingham. But for the untimely death on January 1st of Ald. Frank Moles he too would have received the honour.

Ald. Stanley L. Bowyer

Leonard G. Smalley

March 15th

A tree of the Sophora Japonica species (known as the Chinese Scholar tree) was planted at the boundary of the pitch and putt course on Elms Field, Wokingham formerly launching the borough's contribution to the national *Plant a Tree '73* scheme.

March 15th

Major John Lycett Wills was appointed 18th High Steward of Wokingham.

Major John Lycett Wills (1910-1999)

1973 - 1973

March 23rd

At 8.00 a.m. the automatic telephone exchange took over from the manual and West Forest exchanges. Some 7,000 subscribers were affected, the bulk of them being on the West Forest mobile exchange. The new numbers were six-figure ranging from 78 0000 to 78 787499.

Manual Telephone exchange

March 23rd

A new coach presented to Wokingham St. John Ambulance Brigade by Wokingham Round Table was dedicated by the Rev. Kenneth Martin, Rector of All Saints' Church. A new ambulance was also dedicated outside St. John Headquarters in Goodchild Road.

April 1st

Wokingham's new car parking scheme came into effect making motorists liable to pay for parking for the first time in the four council car parks. Drivers using the Rose Street, Denmark Street, Easthampstead Road off Cockpit Path car parks had to pay 5p for a period up to two hours, or 10p for any period over that in any one day. Parking was free on Sundays and between 6 p.m. and 8 a.m. on all other days.

May

Alderman Stanley Bowyer (1907-1988) was elected as the last Borough Mayor of the old Borough Council.

1973 - 1973

May 23rd

The old Palmer School in Palmer School Road was closed.

The old Palmer School

June

Drivers were warned that parking space in Wokingham's off-street car parks was no longer free. Unless drivers purchased a ticket from the "Trust the Motorist" machine and displayed it in a prominent position on their windscreens they would be liable to a fine of 50p.

June

Estate agents, said to be instructed by a leading property development company, asked Wokingham Borough Council if they would consider disposing of the Town Hall for future development.

October 16th

The Palmer Church of England Junior School in Norreys Avenue was formally opened. Mr. T. D. Whitfield, the Director of Education for Berkshire, unveiled a plaque to commemorate the official opening. Also present were parents and the Mayor and Mayoress of Wokingham, Ald. S. Bowyer and Mrs. J. Foreman-Brown,

November

Wokingham's first railway station was replaced by a low flat-roofed structure.

1974 - 1974

November 16th

The headmistress of Holt School, Miss C Holland, told parents and former pupils at the certificate ceremony that the change-over from grammar to comprehensive would begin in September of the following year when the first year forms would comprise 180 girls from a certain area instead of having qualified in a selective process.

November 29th

Petrol rationing began and thousands of motorists were expected to call at sub-post offices, post offices and special centres throughout Berkshire and South Oxfordshire to collect their petrol ration coupons.

1974

The 16th century, Grade II, *Littlecourt*, formerly *Woodlands*, Reading Road, originally part of Bêches Manor, passed from Berkshire County Council, who had purchased it in 1970, to the Wokingham and District Association for the Elderly, a registered charity founded by Jean Davy, a former Mayor of Wokingham.

16th century Littlecourt, formerly Woodlands
courtesy Wokingham Times

February

Approval for a new boys' hostel to be built in Wokingham was given by Berkshire's Finance Committee. The approval was subject to agreement by the County Council. The idea was to rebuild Green Field House Hostel in Maidenhead on the sites of the Field House and South Field hostels in

1974 - 1974

Wokingham. The cost of about £200,000 would largely be paid for from the sale of the Maidenhead site.

March 31st

At midnight on Sunday 31st March, a three-tier structure came into being; Berkshire County Council became the senior authority; the new Wokingham District Council became responsible for an area roughly similar to that of the Domesday hundred of Charlton; the Wokingham Town Council was formed into a parish council the leader of which retained the courtesy title of Mayor. Queen Elizabeth II authorised Wokingham Town Council to 'bear and use' a Coat of Arms; the Coat of Arms that had been granted to the Borough Council continued to be used.

April

Wokingham Lions Club was founded.

April

Bowyer Crescent was named after Alderman Stanley Bowyer in gratitude for his help in the development of the 800-house Ashridge Park housing estate on Warren House Road.

April 18th

Marion Fergusson-Kelly started an appeal to send books and magazines etc to British soldiers serving in Northern Ireland.

May 9th

The Council began to demolish two Westende Almshouses, formerly owned by Wokingham United Charities Trust. There was an exchange of property, with the Trust gaining some council-owned land on the corner of London Road and Peach Streets for the almshouses.

May 18th

A new extension to Wokingham Methodist church was formally opened by Mrs. Edna Wendt who cut the ribbon across the new doorway. The service was conducted by the Superintendent Minister Dr. Ronald Ashman, the Rev. Wendt and the Rev. Ralph Bates, Minister from 1962 to 1965.

1974 - 1974

June 1st

Mrs. Jean Davy, Chairman of WADE, formally opened *Littlecourt*, Wokingham Day Centre-for the Elderly, which cost f40,000. Some of the money was donated by the then Wokingham Borough Council, Wokingham Rural District Council and Berkshire County Council. The rest came from the people of Wokingham.

June 8th

Wokingham Carnival was organised by the West Forest Round Tablers, who had asked all who participated to follow a medieval theme. A highlight was the medieval tournament complete with the clashing of swords and the expert use of lances as armoured knights on horseback charged their opponents.

July 13th

A hot air balloon was one of the many attractions at the golden jubilee garden party given by the Cinema and Television Benevolent Fund in aid of the home at Glebelands for former artists of stage and screen. Among those present were Sylvia Simms, Jane Seymour and Dame Anna Neagle.

September 3rd

Westende Junior School, Seaford Road, was formally opened as a co-educational junior school with Mr. C. Cunningham-Burley as head teacher. The school came into being because of overcrowding at Wescott Road Primary School (now Wescott Infant School).

September 12th

Westende Old People's Home was officially opened by Mr. Leonard Hackett, Chairman of the National Association of Almshouses.

December

Pottery dating as far back as the 12th century and evidence of cottages from the 14th century were found by members of the Berkshire Archaeological Society in Cross Street where it linked with Peach and Rose Streets.

1975 - 1975

December 13th

The Wokingham annual window-dressing competition took place. Judges invited by the Chamber of Trade inspected shop windows for attractiveness, colour and originality. Professional and non-professional window dressing was taken into account and prizes were awarded for both sections. The judges who included the Mayor and Mayoress, Cllr. and Mrs. John Tattersall found their task difficult but enjoyable. A new entry was a bar at The Olde Rose Inne in the Market Place in which the efforts of two charming "Molly Mogs" won a special prize. Other winners were the *Wokingham Times* Jill Russell, and Esquire, who were presented with their awards by the Mayor and Mayoress.

1975

A special court at Windsor decided that Wokingham Town Council could continue to use its Coat of Arms and continue to elect a Mayor and Mace Bearer.

January

Wokingham railway station was awarded second prize in the Southern Region's Best Kept Stations competition. Each station was judged for its cleanliness and tidiness and Wokingham came second in the Ascot area, with Windsor and Eton Riverside in first place and Camberley third.

Wokingham Railway Station

31st January

Pottery finds dating back to the 13th century and indications of a cottage of that date were discovered at Cross Street and Peach Street where development was scheduled to take place.

1975 - 1975

February

St. Paul's Infant School moved from Shute End to a site adjoining St. Paul's Junior C. of E. School in Oxford Road. The clock tower, school buildings and parish rooms were eventually sold to Berkshire County Council.

February 15th

At the Area Conference at Eastbourne the Wokingham Branch of the Royal British Legion was again presented with the Cayley Cup and the South Eastern Area Merit Cup. Both cups were awarded for its endeavours in respect of the Poppy Appeal and benevolent work. The Branch Chairman, Mr. Albert Dunham, was awarded an Area Certificate of Appreciation that was also presented at Eastbourne.

March

A petition deploring the disgraceful state of Wokingham Market Place was raised by Mr. Ernest Bland, former Mayor of the Borough who delivered it to Wokingham District Council. He described the area as resembling a slum.

April

After the petition was delivered to Wokingham District Council by Mr. Ernest Bland, new covers replaced the dirty, torn ones on the market stalls and quotations for repairing bent and cracked stall tubing were sought.

July

The Guide Dogs for the Blind Association purchased Folly Court in Barkham Road to make way for a complex of buildings for the Wokingham Training Centre for Guide Dogs.

Folly Court House before being demolished

1976 - 1976

July

Wokingham Town Council agreed to contribute £40,000 towards a sports hall at St. Crispin's School, with the understanding that it could be used after school hours by the public. The overall cost of the improvements, modifications and additions to the hall to make it suitable for adult use was £120,000.

September 15th

Wokingham Masonic Temple in Reading Road was dedicated by R.W. Bro. Brig. E.W.C. Flavell, D.S.O., M.C., T.D., Di., Prov. G.M.

November 25th

Berkshire County Council's development committee gave outline planning consent for the proposed sports complex at St. Crispin's School after it had heard that the main problems had been settled at a meeting between Wokingham District and Town Councils.

It had been hoped to build the sports hall complex without disturbing the all-weather tennis/football pitches and by retaining much of the Wokingham Road frontage. However, it was found that there was no alternative but to build on part of the tennis/netball pitches and the frontage of the school. The swimming pool, which was to be constructed at a much later date, would occupy part of the all-weather pitches. By taking this course, the Council hoped that phase one of the scheme—to build two halls and ancillary accommodation—would proceed at an early date.

1976

The Kings Head, a 16th century inn in the Market Place, was demolished to make way for shops and offices.

K&H Construction commenced refurbishment of Nos.22-28 Denmark Street, formerly the home of Teakle Stonemasons.

Taylor Woodrow Homes Ltd. appealed against a decision by Wokingham District Council to refuse permission to build houses. The company claimed that the proposed development would assist first-time buyers.

1976 - 1976

February

It was announced that Pay and Display car parks at Rose Street, Denmark Street, Cockpit Path and Easthampstead Road were to be taken over by Wokingham District Council when the Royal British Legion's three-year lease expired in June. A spokesman for the British Legion Attendants' Company said that the Legion was losing £100 every week on these car parks.

March

Wokingham Railway Station was judged one of the best-kept stations in the Southern Region's South Western Division. The station was awarded a prize for being the best-kept in the Feltham area.

April

Wokingham District Councillor John English informed the Council's Community Services Committee that the Emm Brook at Wokingham was now completely dead because of severe oil pollution and other factors.

May

Wokingham District Council engaged architects to prepare alternative schemes based on the Council's development brief for the Drill Hall site at Denmark Street. It would take approximately four months to prepare the alternative schemes which would then be presented to the Council, after which there would be a period of public consultation.

May 2nd

New lifting barriers were brought into use at the level crossing outside Wokingham Railway Station. The barriers were push-button and controlled from the signal box, and would speed up the flow of road traffic.

June

Around the World in Eighty Days was the theme of the year's Wokingham Carnival and the organisers, West Forest Round Table, said that it had been a winning idea and had helped to make the event the most successful ever with a profit of over £2,000.

1977 - 1977

October 16th

The steam fair at Wokingham Carnival Field failed to attract the public despite attractions including merry-go-rounds, roundabouts and can-can girls.

1977

Work commenced to develop Woose Hill estate.

EMI, the owners of the Ritz cinema in Finchampstead Road, sold the cinema to Jora Leisure. The price was not revealed. Jora planned to transform the cinema into a leisure centre for hire to various groups and organisations.

The Wokingham Society published *A Chronology* compiled by the History Group of the Society.

May 12th

Princess Alexandra, Patron of the Guide Dogs for the Blind Association, formally opened the new training centre at Folly Court, Barkham Road. The Princess was welcomed by the Earl of Lanesborough, President of the Association. The cost of the Centre was £1 million raised by subscription.

June

A plaque was unveiled at Glebelands Rest Home to the memory of Sir Stanley Baker, actor and producer, who had recently died and who had worked for many years to raise money for its upkeep and maintenance. Those present included his widow, Harry Secombe and Sir James Carraras.

1978 - 1978

June 7th

Wokingham celebrated the Queen's Silver Jubilee. Entertainment was provided by local groups and organisations. The highlight was the procession through the town, led by the Arborfield Pipe band and the Jubilee Queen, Miss Nicola King, with her attendants from the Youth Centre in Broad Street, to the Wokingham Town Football Ground in Finchampstead Road. The programme reflected the theme of Accent of Youth.

November

Permission was given by Wokingham Town Council Finance and General Purposes Committee for the Town Council to hold a weekly lottery with a first prize of £1,000. Even if some people did not win a prize they would eventually benefit because profits from the lottery were to be used to finance various Council services. The lottery was scheduled to begin later that month with tickets costing twenty pence each.

November

The old Palmer School in Rectory Road was demolished to make way for old people's accommodation.

December 17th

Wokingham was twinned with Erftstadt. The twinning was symbolised by an exchange of charters.

1978

St. Crispin's sports centre was opened.

1978 - 1978

Queen Victoria House in Peach Street, built 91 years previously to commemorate Queen Victoria's Golden Jubilee celebration in 1887, was demolished to make way for development.

Queen Victoria House prepared for demolition

September 25th

An arsonist set fire to 'Help the Aged' building in Wellington Road and the Old Brewery in Denmark Street that was to be demolished to make way for the Tesco supermarket development.

October 21st

The men of the Royal Electrical and Mechanical Engineers whose headquarters were at Arborfield Garrison were made Honorary Townspeople of Wokingham.

The REME on parade in Broad Street

1979 - 1981

November

Permission was given by Wokingham Town Council Finance and General Purposes Committee for the Town Council to hold a weekly lottery, with a first prize of £1,000. Even if some people did not win a prize they would eventually benefit because profits from the lottery were to be used to finance various Council services. The lottery was scheduled to begin later that month with tickets costing twenty pence each.

1979

Wokingham Brewery and the Drill Hall were demolished to make way for a Tesco Superstore and multi-storey car park.

Wokingham's Indoor Swimming Movement (S.W.I.M.) was founded.

March

Proposals for the creation of three new parishes: Wokingham Without, Arborfield and Barkham were accepted at a W.D.C. meeting.

September 13th

At a ceremony Mr. William R. van Straubenzee M.B.E., M.P. was made Honorary Freeman of the town of Wokingham.

1981

The inner distribution road had been estimated to cost more than one million pounds but Berkshire County Council's three-year capital programme showed that there were no contingencies for it in the following financial year (May 1882-83).

Plans for a railway station at Emmbrook were displayed.

Plans were put forward for a northern bypass to enable the closure of Peach Street and Denmark Street to traffic.

The 1st Woosehill Scout group was formed.

February 2nd

The charity commissioners approved a transfer of trusteeship from the trustees of Wokingham Memorial Clinic in Denmark Street to the Red Cross Association.

1981 - 1981

February

Councillor Jean Davy and Miss Evelyn Ward were awarded M.B.E.s for services to the community and for services to Wokingham Memorial Orthopaedic Clinic respectively. Miss Ward died before she could receive her award.

Cllr. Jean Marjorie Davy (1915-1987)

April

Wokingham Mayor Cllr. Mrs Marion Fergusson Kelly made a flying visit to Northern Ireland to see British soldiers at work. Her two-day whistle-stop tour began with a visit to Army headquarters in Northern Ireland, at Lisburn, where she also presented a Long Service and Good Conduct Medal to Sergeant Bryan Probert.

April 12th

The *Ritz* Cinema re-opened after being closed for almost two years. The final bill for the *Ritz Entertainment Centre* rose to £150,000—50% more than the original estimates. The manager, Ray Hipkin said that work would be completed on Good Friday.

June

Cecil Nibbs, Wokingham Town Hall Mace Bearer for 22 years, died.

June

Wokingham District Council proposed to build a civic complex costing £5 million. This was to be funded by the disposal of property in Wellington Road and Denmark Street. Mr. Heseltine, Environmental Secretary, refused planning permission.

June 13th

Wokingham and Bracknell M.P. William van Straubenzee was awarded a knighthood in the Queen's Birthday Honours List. He was honoured for political services in his 22nd year as a Member of Parliament.

1981 - 1981

July 31st

St. Anne's Nursing Home off London Road closed and the community of seven Bon Secour nuns left after having run the home since 1939. They had to sell the house because of soaring bills, and work on the A329M extension threatened the future of the rest home.

September 8th

Hawthorns Primary School, Northway, Woosehill, Wokingham was formally opened with forty-eight children under Mrs. Fawcett, Headmistress.

Hawthorn Primary School   © Jim Bell

October

Cantley Country Club re-opened as a hotel thanks to the intervention of two businessmen, Mr. Leo Ratcliffe, a businessman in the motor trade and Mr. Maurice Monk, a country club manager, who obtained a lease with their own cash.

Cantley House Hotel
Courtesy Cantley House Hotel

1982 - 1983

November 5th

Mr. Heseltine, Environmental Secretary, ordered the council to release an extra 1,000 acres of land for building over the next four years.

1982

South Place, a row of cottages built in the late 18th century as Wokingham's first silk factory, was demolished and replaced by a block of offices.

Wokingham Town Football Club won the Isthmian League Division 1 Championship.

1983

Furious debates took place over the development of *Heseltown* in areas adjacent to Wokingham. (Mr. Heseltine, First Secretary of State, tried to force an additional 8,000 houses on central Berkshire which became known as Heseltown.)

January 4th

Town Mayor Cllr. David Ireland awarded the *Wokingham Cup* to the REME soldiers serving in Northern Ireland in recognition of the excellent work they had done there on behalf of this country.

January 31st

Town Mayor, Cllr. David Ireland officially opened the modernised offices of the Citizens' Advice Bureau in the Town Hall.

February 28th

The Acorn Cup was returned to Wokingham by Canon John Lawton. This Cup was originally presented to Captain James Webb, Commander of the Loyal Association, by the townspeople of Wokingham on July 28th 1802 for his part in protecting Wokingham during hostilities between Britain and France in the French Revolutionary Wars (see Page 1).

Canon John Lawton passes the Acorn Cup to Mayor Cllr. David Ireland
courtesy Wokingham Times

1983 - 1983

April 19th

The Courtyard Market in the Town Hall was officially opened by the Town Mayor, Cllr. David Ireland, when he welcomed stall-holders and shoppers. The market area was open for four days a week—Tuesdays, Thursdays, Fridays and Saturdays. During the evenings it was available for hire for public and private functions. For evening functions the height of the stalls was adjustable and could be assembled to form a stage.

The Mayor, Cllr. David Ireland opens the Courtyard Market
courtesy Wokingham Times

May

An inspector from the Department of the Environment announced that, despite objections from the town and district councils, the Halifax Building Society would be allowed to open an office in Gotelee House in the Market Place. Some saw this as a signal for building societies and estate agents to flood the town, while others welcomed the increased opportunity for savings and borrowing.

June

The refurbished Old Forge in Peach Street became the premises of supermarket chain SavaCentre at a formal opening attended by the Mayor and Mayoress, Cllr. David Ireland and his wife Janet.

The refurbished forge
© Jim Bell

1984 - 1985

September 17th

Woolworth's in Peach Street was badly damaged by fire. which also threatened nearby residents. The store was closed to customers for a week while staff salvaged stock and cleaned up. The company's press officer could not say how long it would be before the store would re-open.

October

Suffolk Lodge Care Home in Rectory Road was opened by Mayor, Cllr. David Ireland. The Lodge was built by W.E. Chivers and run by Berkshire Social Services.

1984

Rose Street residents objected to the intrusion of businesses into the historic street.

July 1st.

At a garden party held at WADE, Little Court, Reading Road the Deputy Lieutenant of Berkshire, Mr. Lewis Moss, formally opened an extension to the building.

August 28th

Television star Hannah Gordon formally opened Safeways Supermarket in Woosehill.

September

Comedian Ernie Wise volunteered his services free to star with a cast of eleven children from Emmbrook School in a five-minute film by the Keep Berkshire Tidy Group.

September 27th

The new Red Cross Centre in Denmark Street was formally opened by Lady Victoria Palmer, patron of the Berkshire Red Cross Society.

October 6th

Men of the R.E.M.E. marched through Wokingham with bayonets .fixed to celebrate the anniversary of being granted the status of Honorary Townspeople of Wokingham.

1985

March

The Wokingham Players were given permission by Wokingham District Council to build a £150,000 theatre at Cantley Estate.

May

A major event entitled *Wokingham Act Wild* took place in Wokingham to help local residents appreciate the countryside around them. It comprised a series of exhibitions and talks and was organised by the WERD the (Wokingham Environmental Resources Development) team. The team worked from the teachers' centre in Alderman Willey Close and was funded by the Manpower Services Commission.

May 8th

Wokingham Town Council celebrated V.E. (Victory in Europe) Day. A thanksgiving concert was held at Westende School to commemorate 40 years of peace. It was an opportunity for ex-servicemen and war widows to revive the songs, music and memories of the Second World War.

June 8th/9th

The Wokingham Carnival took to the town streets and fields at the weekend. From early afternoon until the evening thousands of people enjoyed the festivities. Highlights included parachutists from R.E.M.E. spectacularly landing on a field in front of the spectators. More than 20 floats gathered to be judged by Miss Wokingham and the Mayor, Cllr. Keith Cattran, before setting off for a grand procession through the town centre. The profits helped to raise cash for the Guide Dogs for the Blind Training Centre at Folly Court.

August

During a special visit from the 1st Battalion, The Duke of Edinburgh's Royal Regiment, lunchtime shoppers in the Market Place were treated to a display of military music and marching from the regimental band and corps of drums. Among those present were the Mayor Cllr. Keith Cattran and Deputy Mayor Mrs. Margaret Busst.

August

Wokingham Town Council accepted a tender for the landscaping of Howard Palmer Park for which it had allocated £32,000 from the annual

1985 - 1985

budget. Some extra items were added including five lamp posts in a mock Victorian style with reinforced glass and photo sensitive cells.

October

Edward Court Hotel in Wellington Road was officially opened by the town Mayor, Cllr. Keith Cattran, and Mrs. Cattran, the Mayoress. The hotel had 25 bedrooms all with en suite bathrooms and was owned by Luff Building of Wokingham. This was the first time the company had run a hotel.

November 2nd

A *Victorian Day* was held, with many people in costume, to celebrate 100 years of the creation of the borough. As part of the celebrations the Lord Lieutenant of Berkshire, the Hon. Gordon Palmer, planted a mulberry tree commemorating the legendary association of the tree with the former silk industry of the town.

A steamer fire engine on display on Victorian Day
© Jim Bell

1986 - 1986

1986

Work commenced to develop Glebelands housing estate.

Cantley House Estate in Milton Road was purchased by the District Council for use as a public open space.

Cllr. Jean Marjorie Davy and Veronica Muriel Essame (1906-1993) were made Honorary Townpersons of the town of Wokingham.

February

Douglas Fielding and June Brown, also known as Sergeant Quick and Dot Cotton from television's *East Enders* opened the *Ritz Bingo Club* that had just undergone a refurbishment costing £150,000.

April 4th

A plaque was unveiled at WADE Centre by Major John L. Wills, High Steward of Wokingham, to honour Jean Davy MBE JP who founded Wokingham and District Association for the Elderly in December 1968.

September 21st

Anthony Cross died. His first love was history, and development in Wokingham in the 1960s sparked off an endeavour to try to save the town from planners. This led to him founding the Wokingham Society in 1964. He was its leading force and chairman for ten years and its president for twelve.

1987 - 1987

October 5th

The new Wokingham Theatre at Cantley was opened by comedian Beryl Reid O.B.E. and television star Hughie Green. After nearly forty years of entertaining local audiences, beginning with its first performance in the Masonic Hall in 1948, Wokingham Theatre at last had a permanent home.

Wokingham Theatre © Jim Bell

December 11th

Berkshire County Council agreed plans to build a full circular inner distribution road at a cost of £7.9 million.

1987

Work commenced to build new council offices at Shute End. Part of the new building would comprise part of the first Rectory of St. Paul's Parish Church built in 1867 and paid for by John Walter III.

Work was due to commence on a link road between Wiltshire and London Roads to enable traffic to drive directly to London Road.

March 13th

Princess Diana visited Dr. Barnardo's High Close School escorted by Col. the Hon. Gordon Palmer, Lord Lieutenant of Berkshire. After she had been introduced to the local dignitaries she chatted to the parents. After the visit she made an unscheduled walkabout to talk to the crowds outside.

1987 - 1987

Princess Diana visits the arts and crafts room
courtesy Wokingham Times

May

Sir William van Straubenzee, M.P. of Wokingham for nearly twenty-eight years, retired from politics.

May 28th

A poll was taken on the proposed inner distribution road. There were eight polling stations.

June

John Redwood, Wokingham's new Conservative MP, swept to victory in the General Election. He won with a comfortable majority over his closest rival John Leston, Liberal.

courtesy Sir John Redwood

June 6th

Wokingham celebrated a decade of twinning with Erfstadt. Wokingham Round Table and Beazer Homes organised the carnival and hoped that the event had raised the Twinning Association's profile in the town. The excellent standard of floats showed the amount of hard work that had gone into them.

1988 - 1988

1988

Various plans for the improvement of the Market Place were studied. The cost to Wokingham Town Council was estimated to be £5,000 and to the District Council, £79,000. The plans included the conversion of the Paddocks into a car park, and the construction of an access road through the middle of Elms Field. The plans were approved.

Plans for the construction of a shop and office complex on land between Rose and Broad Streets were approved

Following the outcome of the poll held in May approval was given to the construction of the inner distribution road.

January

The people of Wokingham agreed to twinning with the French town of Viry-Chatillon.

March

Town Mayor Cllr. John Green and Deputy Mayor, Cllr. Fred Clark spent a weekend in Viry-Chatillon. Unfortunately, a previous attempt to link Wokingham and Viry-Chatillon had ended in disaster when a member of the Twinning Association, likened Viry-Chatillon to Fulham or Wandsworth.

June

Hundreds of revellers dressed up as their favourite film and cartoon characters to make the 8th annual carnival one of the biggest. Overcast skies and strong winds were not enough to spoil the day for around 6,000 people who cheered the floats through the town and followed them on to Cantley Field for an afternoon of fun. The finale was provided by the Auto Space Kings and their daring motorbike display on a wire 60 feet above the ground.

June 26th

The Twinning links between Wokingham and Viry Chatillon were made official.

July 9th

After renovation Emmbrook Village Hall was officially opened by Wokingham Town Mayor Cllr, Fred Clark.

1989 - 1989

Emmbrook Village Hall © Jim Bell

August

Stakis St Anne's Manor Hotel, formerly St. Anne's Manor, was formally opened on London Road after a restoration costing £9 million.

September

Wokingham Town Hall underwent a major series of repairs, including work on the stonework.

November 21st

Plans to build a car park at the Paddocks at Elms Field were agreed by Wokingham District councillors. The decision was condemned by local residents who were angry at the loss of green land near their homes.

1989

Work commenced to develop Keep Hatch Housing Estate.

A compulsory purchase was announced of 279 plots and properties in Wokingham for the inner distribution road.

January

Wokingham farmer Mark Hall sold Heathlands Country Market and Garden Centre to Cramphorn Plc based in Chelmsford, Essex, for £1.3 million.

March

Stanley Bowyer left hundreds of pounds' worth of legacies to various Wokingham charities and organisations including £500 to All Saints' Church; £250 each to Westende Charities, Wokingham, to be used for the

1989 - 1989

residents and matron; the Wokingham and Bracknell Royal Naval Association; MENCAP; the Berkshire British Legion No.3 Group of which he was president; and the Winnersh British Legion Poppy Fund.

March 8th

It was feared that the Wokingham Society would be forced to close when only thirteen members attended the annual general meeting. The threat of closure was lifted when many more members attended the next AGM.

June 19th

Many people attended the Wokingham Carnival organised by Wokingham Round Table who had resolved to donate the proceeds to the Wokingham Adult Training Centre in Woosehill Lane. The day started with floats assembling in Norreys Avenue to be judged. Among the judges were Wokingham's British pairs ice skating champions Cheryl Peake and Andrew Naylor. The procession, headed by the St. Sebastian Wokingham band, arrived at Cantley for Olympic silver medallist swimmer Sharon Davies to open the Carnival There were many stalls in Cantley Field manned by volunteers from charities and voluntary groups from the district.

June 21st

H.R.H. Princess Anne, the Princess Royal, formally opened the new offices of Wokingham District Council at Shute End. After a brief tour of the building, the Princess Royal signed the visitors' book in front of a small crowd inside the council chamber. Major Douglas Goddard, chairman of Wokingham District Council, thanked the Princess Royal for signing a photograph of herself which was hung in the chamber.

Princess Anne unveils the commemorative plaque
courtesy Wokingham Times

1989 - 1989

August

Wokingham town councillors overwhelmingly supported a recommendation to seek urgent talks to save Martin's Pool. Town Mayor Cllr. Fred Clark led a four-man delegation to meet members of Wokingham District Council in a final attempt to save the pool.

October

After standing empty for two years, the *Bull and Bush* Inn was converted into a shopping mall named *Bush Walk*.

The Bush Hotel ready to be demolished
courtesy Goatley Collection

Bush Walk courtesy Goatley collection

1990 - 1990

October 30th

At a full meeting of Wokingham District Council, Cllr. Keith Malvern presented a petition containing 6,196 signatures of people who did not want Martin's Pool to be closed to Council chairman Douglas Goddard. Conservative councillors however were adamant that the town could not support two swimming pools.

December 5th

The foundation stone of Wokingham's new cancer care day centre at Wokingham Hospital, Barkham Road, was laid by British Airways' chairman Lord King.

1990

Cllr. John Green's agent mislaid the councillor's nomination papers for the district council elections in May. A search was made but the papers could not be found in time.

January

Wokingham District Council held a further ballot on the inner distribution road. The project survived by one vote.

February

Wokingham's modernised Market Place was expected to be completed by the beginning of April. Subsequently the outdoor market had to move temporarily to the new pedestrian area behind the Town Hall.

February

Winds of 80mph swept through the district of Wokingham closing schools, blacking out villages and leaving homes and buildings damaged. The London Weather Centre forecast that there was more to come.

February 22nd

The owner of the *Ritz* cinema decided to close it down in May because of competition from *The Point*, a new screen complex at Skimped Hill in Bracknell that was due to open in April.

March

Plans to build Wokingham Carnival Pool were approved.

1990 - 1990

March

Wilfred Bailey and Son's bakery, owned by the family since the late 1970s, was sold to John Williams, a departmental manager at Sainsbury. The branches of the bakery were located in Wokingham, Crowthorne, Woodley, Lower Earley and Reading. The business in Wokingham was started in 1931 by Charles Lee (1870-1934) and Wilfred Bailey joined the company and purchased it when Don Lee, the proprietor, retired from the business.

April

Lady Elizabeth Godsal was nominated to be the next High Sheriff of Berkshire. She succeeded Raymond Seymour of Bucklebury, Reading, and would be the first woman High Sheriff of Berkshire. Her husband Alan held the post in 1959.

Lady Elizabeth Godsal

May

The *Ritz* Cinema was to remain open for as long as it was viable according to the owner. Although he was applying for planning permission to change its use it did not follow that it would definitely close. The cinema was still provisionally scheduled for closure when *The Point* in Bracknell opened.

May

St. Paul's Parish Church congregation won their battle to build parish rooms to provide meeting places for local organisations. They feared, however, that the delay in taking the application to a Government inspector would increase the final bill.

August

Wokingham's new £4.8 million swimming pool was approved. In a vote taken behind closed doors the district council recreation committee agreed to enter into a contract with Laing Wessex on behalf of John Laing Construction Ltd. to build the new pool and related road works.

1990 - 1990

September

According to an annual inspection carried out by chartered surveyors Wokingham Town Hall had 62 structural faults: 46 interior and 16 exterior problems which included damp, loose mortar and a collapsed kitchen ceiling. Town councillors instructed the town clerk to proceed with the urgent repairs.

September

Westmead Day Centre staff and friends celebrated its first birthday. The Centre, in Rances Lane, was converted from the former Westmead School which catered for disabled children. When the children were transferred to the Whitelocke Infant and Palmer Junior Schools the adults took the opportunity to use a building that was virtually purpose-built for their needs.

September 3rd

Whitelocke School in Norreys Avenue, won a five-year battle to integrate disabled and able-bodied children. After years of disappointment school staff and parents were overjoyed to learn that building had finally started on their new nursery.

September 10th

Prince William's first term commenced at Ludgrove School. He arrived accompanied by his parents Prince Charles and Princess Diana to be greeted by the head master, Nichol Marston, and the school staff.

Prince William being greeted by headmaster Nichol Marston
Courtesy Wokingham Times

1991 - 1991

October

John and Rosemary Lea of The Wokingham Society launched a book entitled *Wokingham—A Pictorial History*. They were members of the History Group of the Society and with their fellow-members they collected 163 old photographs and produced a narrative about the town, the personalities and the changes that took place in the town between the 1890s and the 1950s. The book was published at the end of October.

November 13th

Wokingham new cancer care centre, British Airways MacMillan House in Barkham Road, was formally opened by Lord King of Wartnaby, chairman of British Airways which donated towards the building costs.

1991

Malcolm Rifkin, the Secretary of State for Transport, was given a tour of Wokingham to enable him to consider the necessity for the inner distribution road.

Work commenced to build parish rooms for St. Paul's Parish Church in Reading Road.

February

Heavy snow and arctic temperatures left Wokingham rail commuters stranded; schools closed; refuse collection services abandoned; and hospital casualty units working at full stretch. It was estimated that costs to keep the roads clear reached £250,000,

February

Mayor Cllr. Fred Clark was granted his own Scout group. The Mayor's troop had been disbanded after the first and fifth troops had amalgamated to become the Third Wokingham Troop.

1991 - 1991

February 18th

Work started to construct the new £5 million Wokingham swimming pool in Wellington Road when district council chairman, Jean Meyers, dug the first official hole. It was hoped that the pool would be finished by August 1992.

March

The people of Wokingham were scheduled to vote on the future of Martin's Pool on Monday April 15th. Wokingham District Council which owned the pool had no alternative but to hold the poll after it was demanded at a town meeting.

April 11th

Berkshire's new High Sheriff, Lewis Moss of Queensmere, Sandhurst Road, Wokingham, was due to be sworn in for his term of office at a special inauguration ceremony at Reading Magistrates Court. His predecessor was Lady Elizabeth Godsal.

April 15th

The people of Wokingham voted in favour of retaining Martin's Pool. Those who voted to keep the pool numbered 3,255. Those against numbered 83 against, a majority of 3,172. And 3,201 voted against selling the pool site for development with 88 in favour. Unfortunately the vote was ignored by the Borough Council.

May

Wokingham Football Club put its ground in Finchampstead Road up for sale to major developers in an attempt to find a buyer to ease debts estimated at over £100,000 and rising.

August 15th

The Pet Shop in Peach Street, originally called "Henry Bowyer & Son Corn Chandlers" when it opened in 1926, was due to close down on Saturday August 17th with the owner of the property, Michael Bowyer, stating that for him the business was no longer viable. Subsequently on Friday the business side of it was sold to Richard Croyden of Woosehill, with Michael Bowyer retaining ownership of the property.

1991 - 1991

The Pet Shop
© Jim Bell

October 17th

BBC Gardeners' Question Time was recorded in St. Crispin's Sports Hall with members of the Wokingham Horticultural Association providing the questions.

November

The Wokingham Chronicle ceased publication, ending an unsuccessful two-year long attempt to establish a foothold in the town. Launched with a banner headline "We're here to stay," the newspaper finally gave up the unequal struggle.

November 3rd

The Parish Rooms of St. Paul's Parish Church were formally opened and dedicated by John, Bishop of Reading.

St. Paul's Parish Rooms © Jim Bell

1992 - 1992

December 6th

Soldiers began to vacate Arborfield Garrison and a last passing out parade was held to mark the occasion. Defence cuts had decreed that the Training Battalion and Depot, with permanent staff and around 300 recruits, would have to close down. The departing battalion moved to its new home in Pirbright, Surrey. The company would then be known as Rowecroft Company. The R.E.M.E. staff band remained at Arborfield.

1992

Langborough Recreation Ground for organised sports was opened.

Plans were approved for a shopping development at 19-21 Market Place.

March

Wokingham Baptist Church in Milton Road planned to exhume 150 graves to accommodate a new hall. The remains were to be reburied at the Wokingham Free Church Cemetery unless relatives wished to make other arrangements.

April

Wokingham's new leisure centre was to be called *The Carnival Pool* and was expected to be finished slightly ahead of the scheduled date of September 14th and be open to the public towards the end of October.

April

Emmbrook Women's Institute was forced to close down because no one would volunteer to be secretary. Emmbrook W.I. was formed in October 1936 and survived many difficult times, including the war years when the A.R.P. took over the hall and members met in the Baptist Room in Milton Road.

May

Berkshire County Council sold Oakfield House in Barkham Road to an undisclosed buyer for over £625,000, although it was to remain as a nursing home. The land had been declared surplus to requirements in the previous June despite protests from relatives and friends of the 26 elderly residents who feared the move would be too much for them to bear. Nevertheless the Council had pressed ahead with its plans to close the home to release funds to upgrade other social services' homes.

1992 - 1992

Oakfield House
© Bella Acki

May 3rd

Town Macebearer Albert Dunham was nominated the official warden of the Guild of Macebearers in the south. This was the first time that Wokingham had been given this honour. Mr. Dunham was reported to be 'as proud as punch'.

Albert Dunham (1922-2007)

May 12th

At Wokingham Mayor Making ceremony retiring High Steward Major John Wills was presented with a plaque bearing the crest of Wokingham Town Council. Lady Elizabeth Godsal his successor was also honoured by being presented with an illuminated copy of the declaration of her acceptance of office.

1992 - 1992

May 18th

Fifty-three members of staff were made redundant at Radyne Holdings in Molly Millar Lane, because of the recession. The company, which made machinery, suffered a serious drop in orders.

June

Former Mayoress of Wokingham, Mabel Perkins celebrated her 100th birthday. She received a telegram from the Queen and another from the Canadian High Commissioner in recognition of the kindness she showed to Canadian soldiers during the Second World War. The Canadian Veterans' Association UK also planned to plant a tree in her honour. Mabel had opened her home in Broad Street to evacuees and Canadian soldiers.

July 10th

Wokingham Mayor, Cllr. Bob Wyatt, and others 'slept rough' in the entrance of Boots Chemist in the Market Place to raise money for CARITAS for the creation of a hostel for the homeless in Wokingham. The sleepers estimated that they raised £300 which brought CARITAS 10% nearer to its target.

September

The contract of Roadrunner Security, the clamping unit hired to operate in Wokingham Library parking area in Broad Street, was not renewed because of their bullying tactics.

September 6th

Martin's Pools were finally closed .in the presence of Tony and Peter Girdler, grandsons of former Councillor and owner William Thomas Martin.

Workmen dismantling one of Martin's pools
courtesy Goatley Collection

1993 - 1993

September 7th

Prince Harry joined his older brother William at Ludgrove School. As a new boy or 'squit', the school's nickname for first year pupils, he was to share a dormitory with other boys and wear a uniform of blue or grey corduroy trousers, blue shirt and blue V-neck sweater. Boarders were permitted three home visits a term.

September 7th

Police ordered Roadrunner Security to release Mrs. Sue Tallent's car which she had parked in front of Wokingham Library beside the wall of the chemist's shop while she went into Montague House to sign on for a college course. Minutes later she emerged to find that her Cavalier car had been clamped. The police received advice from their control room and told the clampers that if they refused to release the car they could be arrested.

October 24th

The Carnival Pool was formally opened. The first swimmer was Bea Snell, better known as Mistress Bet, the dragon cook, of Kentwell Hall. She regularly participated in reconstructions of history in Wokingham and at the old Tudor hall in Long Melford.

Bea Snell

December

A scheme intended to ensure the future of an avenue of lime trees at Langborough recreation ground was set in motion by Mayor Cllr. Bob Wyatt. He turned the soil on the first sapling watched by town councillors and Wokingham M.P. John Redwood.

1993

Plans were approved for the construction of a Waitrose Supermarket in Rose Street.

Plans to build a Tesco supermarket in Finchampstead Road were approved.

1994 - 1994

January 2nd

The Baptist Church in Milton Road was re-opened after being modernised with a new hall and additional offices.

May

After 25 years of controversy, the Inner Distribution Road was finally rejected by the County Council.

May 8th

Wokingham Baptists celebrated the reopening of their church in Milton Road. Approximately 300 people attended a special service of thanksgiving and dedication.

July

Wokingham district councillors agreed to accept an offer for Martin's Pools from the highest bidder. The land was acquired for sheltered housing and the money raised from the sale was estimated to be £500,000.

July 26th

Laing Homes was revealed as the highest bidder for Martin's Pools at a council meeting but the sum that the company was to pay was kept a secret until negotiations had been completed.

September

A celebration plate designed and engraved by disabled teenager Rebecca Gale was presented by Wokingham to the people of Viry Chatillon. The gift marked five years of twinning between the towns and was commissioned by Wokingham's Town Twinning Association .

December 4th

Woosehill Community Centre was officially opened.

December

Protesters finally admitted defeat in the battle to save Martin's Pools after the government refused to intervene. The Department of the Environment announced that it had decided not to call in the planning application. As soon as the decision of the Secretary of State was revealed consent notices for the site clearance and the new housing were issued by Wokingham District Council.

1994

March

Gillet & Johnson completely rebuilt the Wokingham Town Hall clock at a cost of £2,700 and gave it an all-weather varnish. It was now only necessary to move the hands forward and back to adjust it for spring and autumn.

March

The news that Wokingham was to have a new £2.3 million library in Denmark Street was given a warm welcome. As promised, the building was to accommodate additional books and offer more advanced reference facilities than the present one in Montague House. The new library would also become the library headquarters for Wokingham District.

March 11th

The official opening took place of West Oak Nursing Home, Murray Road, which could accommodate 55 residents, The home had been running for a year and was initially built to cater for former patients from Wokingham Hospital.

West Oak Nursing Home
© Jim Bell

April

Work commenced to build houses on the site of former Martin's Pools. The original plan had been to build sheltered housing but the contractor later stated that this was not financially possible and instead built Poppy Place comprising three and four-bedroomed houses.

1994 - 1994

April 12th

Her Majesty the Queen came to Wokingham to visit Glebelands rest home. During her visit she inaugurated two new bungalows, a summer house and gate wings located at the entrance to Glebelands.

June

Burger King was opened at the Carnival Field.

June 5th

The Town Mayor's church parade was held in the evening for the first time.

July

The Metalair building at the corner of Wellington and Station Roads was demolished.

July

Mr. Stanley Harris was awarded a medal for 22 years' service as a traffic warden. He was thrilled that the dedication he had given to his work had been recognised and said, "It's an honour to get the award and I'm very pleased."

Stan Harris receives medal for 22 years' service as a traffic warden.

July

An explosion at Wokingham Station brought rush-hour traffic to a standstill and a bomb squad team was called in. The team discovered that the blast was caused by a minor electrical fault.

July

A bell retrieved 40 years ago from the old Palmer School rang for the first time at the new Palmer School. The bell had almost been forgotten about until headmaster Russell Palmer found it and decided to re-hang it as a tribute to the school's long history. To celebrate the occasion a ceremony was attended by past and present pupils.

July

The Department of the Environment refused to class the old Tythe Barn Hotel in Glebelands Road as a listed building.

Tithe Barn
courtesy Wokingham Times

August 11th

Planners finally struck the death knell for the Tithe Barn in Wokingham. One of the few remaining large historic buildings in the district was to be bulldozed to make way for 18 flats in Glebelands Road.

October 1st

Work commenced to install traffic lights at the junction of Rectory Road and Broad Street.

October 22nd

A lamp that had been installed outside the Roebuck public house 90 years ago was removed because of damage by a passing bus.

1995

January

When the demolition of the old Tithe Barn Hotel in Glebelands Road was taking place the contractors found a large cement block inscribed with a date and some initials. It was assumed that they referred to the date of the

1995 - 1995

erection and the builders of the original building. Messrs Fairbriar decided to include it in the entrance leading into the flats being erected on the site and invited Councillor Mrs Ann Davis as Town Mayor to lay it. It was inscribed, *Presented to the Mayor of Wokingham, Councillor Mrs Ann Davis by Fairbriar Ltd. 17th November 1995.*

January

The traffic lights at the junction of Rectory Road and Broad Street were switched on.

January 10th

At a public meeting in Emmbrook Village Hall after it had been refurbished at a cost of £20,000 town councillors listed several complaints from the public regarding the poor standard of work. The public were then requested to vacate the hall while councillors held a meeting in private to discuss the problems raised. These included leaving hot water pipes exposed after replacing the central heating and failure to fill holes in the walls.

February

January was the wettest January in Wokingham ever recorded according to recordings taken at the Wokingham Meteorological Station at Emmbrook School. The figures indicate that 138.2mm of rain fell during the month—breaking the previous record in 1948 by 10.7mm.

March

Wokingham became a Unitary authority with the demise of Berkshire County Council.

June

There was an outcry over psychic fairs being held in Wokingham Town Hall. The Town Clerk investigated the legality of the fairs and was told by legal experts that the fairs would only have been illegal if there had been an intent to deceive the public.

June

Vandal-proof benches were to be installed in Howard Palmer Park because the park had been the target of hooligans during that year. Tough Plaswood seats were to replace benches which had been badly damaged. Decorative lamps had also suffered, conifer trees were burned down and brick planters defaced. The Town Mayor, Cllr. Ann Davis, also suggested that security lights be erected in the park to deter vandals.

July

The Molly Millar in Station Road was renamed *Big Hand Mo's Goodtime Emporium* after a refurbishment costing £200,000. The new name was part of the refurbishment programme by owners Scottish and Newcastle.

July

After standing derelict for some time the Pin and Bowl public house in Finchampstead Road was demolished.

July 5th

Princess Diana arrived at Ludgrove School to collect her two sons. A police Landrover had already left with the boys' belongings. Shortly afterwards the Princess stopped off at Santram newsagents where she and her sons regularly bought sweets. Prince William left for the last time to start at Eton in the following September.

September

A scroll listing the names of the Wokingham Company of the Royal Berkshire Regiment dating from September 18th 1914 was presented to Mayor Ann Davis on behalf of the Town Council. The scroll had been in safe keeping at the barracks in Slough for 30 years but had to be refurbished by the Council. The Regiment, renamed the Wessex Regiment Territorial Army, decided to return it to its rightful home in Wokingham. It was to be kept in the War Memorial Annexe where it could be seen by the public among the other treasures from Wokingham's past. A small plaque was also included in memory of those who gave their lives for their country in the Second World War (the scroll and plaque originally hung in the Drill Hall).

Cllr. Ann Amanda Davis
(1934-2018)

1995 - 1995

September 16th

A fire destroyed three-quarters of the furniture stored in the storage unit owned by Andy's of Molly Millars Industrial Estate, Fishponds Road. It was estimated that the total loss was less than £100,000. The fire was believed to have been caused by an electrical fault in the heater units.

October

Town Mayor Cllr. Ann Davis and Town Cllr. Keith Malvern unveiled a new sundial in Howard Palmer Park in pouring rain. The pupils of Emmbrook School had won an inter-school competition to design the best sundial, which they had made almost vandal-proof. Instead of a triangular indicator, or gnomon, the shadow was cast by the person wishing to calculate the time. The £11,000 attraction was funded by Wokingham Town Council who said it had a valuable contribution to make to the cultural life of Wokingham.

Sundial
(On a sunny day your shadow will tell the time)
© Jim Bell

October 14th

Wokingham Youth and Community Centre on Reading Road opposite St. Paul's Church was formally opened by County Cllr. George Mair and Kate Higgins, a centre member, on Saturday October 14th. The Centre replaced the old premises located next to the library in Broad Street which had been in use for 24 years. The new Centre provided a place for youngsters to meet and become involved in various activities.

1996 - 1996

Wokingham Youth and Community Centre, Reading Road
© Jim Bell

December 2nd

Many people came to enjoy the Wokingham Winter Carnival. The centre of town was alive with music and laughter. There were numerous clowns, jugglers, and men on stilts. The Victorian market was so popular that it almost blocked the streets. Many of the stalls were collecting for charity. Period costumes could be seen including that of Wokingham's Police Inspector, Paul Cessell, who was strutting around in Victorian policeman's garb complete with top hat. The Wokingham Society Local History Group also wore Dickensian costumes and had an exhibition in the Town Hall. There were 80 floats in the procession including one of Postman Pat followed by the Mayor, Cllr. Ann Davis, the Town Crier and councillors in full ceremonial dress.

1996

March 5th

The Rt. Hon. Virginia Bottomley, Secretary of State for National Heritage, unveiled a plaque in Wokingham's new library in Denmark Street to commemorate the construction of the building.

April 8th

A telephone STD code of 0118 for the Reading area was introduced and was to run in parallel with 01734 until December 31st 1997.

1996 - 1996

April 24th

Wokingham Tourist Information Centre was opened by the Mayor of Wokingham, Cllr. Ann Davis, and Cecil Trembath, Chairman of Berkshire County Council. The scheme which cost around £50,000 was jointly funded by the Town Council and Berkshire County Council.

May 6th

Many people went to the Market Place on Bank Holiday Monday to enjoy Wokingham's first-ever May Fayre extravaganza. There was something for everyone with food, drink, craft stalls, dancing, music, and bonnet competitions. The event was organised by Gerald Aggett, President of Wokingham Lions.

June 1st

A blue plaque was attached to Wokingham Town Hall while another was placed on the NatWest bank building to commemorate Rose Street. The chairman of the Wokingham Society, Donald Macdonald, said that the fruition of the plan was attributed to the group's new treasurer, Roy Thomas. Before plaques could be added to the buildings, Mr. Thomas had to go through a time-consuming planning application process. It was the intention to put plaques on the Queen's Head public house, the oldest house in The Terrace and the Overhangs in Peach Street.

June 30th

Victorian cottages at Nos. 184-186 London Road were demolished to make way for a new housing development. The cottages had stood for decades and had become familiar landmarks in the town. Planners gave permission on June 28th for two four-bedroom houses to be built on the site and the bulldozers came two days later to demolish the cottages.

July

Planners at Wokingham District Council agreed to establish a new conservation area along part of the north and south sides of Langborough Road to protect its Victorian character.

July 2nd

A young persons' hostel in Seaford Court, Wokingham, was officially opened by the Chairman of the Wokingham District Council, Cllr. Diana Carpenter. The hostel accommodated ten homeless young people, aged between 18 and 25, with a view to them finding a job and then their own

1996 - 1996

accommodation. A number of councils and organisations were involved in the building of the hostel but it was the brain child of Chris Pape of Finchampstead Road, who created the Roman Catholic charity CARITAS ('love for all' in Latin).

September 6th

Keep Hatch Manor House in Binfield burned down on Friday evening. Firemen fought the fire for two hours before getting it under control.

October 28th

People waited outside Wokingham's new library in Denmark Street for the officially opening on Monday morning. The new building was four times larger than the previous library at Montague House in Broad Street. The adults and children's lending library accommodated 50,000 new books in addition to the original 40,000. The ground floor featured a quiet reference and local studies area together with IT (Information Technology) facilities, including the internet, and a meeting room which could be hired by the public.

The official opening day of Wokingham Public Library
Left to right: Town Mayor Cllr. Tina Marinos Miller, Cllr. John Trimming, Borough Mayor Cllr. Diana Carpenter and Mr. John Hicks, County Librarian.
© Wokingham Times

1997 - 1997

October 29th

Waitrose opened its doors for the first time at 8.30 am. The first customer received a bouquet of flowers.

November

The *Unsung Heroes* award scheme was introduced by The Town Mayor, Cllr. Tina Marinos Miller, to honour the most hard working and caring members of the community. The awards, which became the main civic function of the year, were a way for the Town Council to say "thank you" to those who had benefitted Wokingham.

December 20th

The end of an era at the Arborfield Army Apprentices College was marked with a special march when the final contingent of REME students to complete a two-year apprenticeship, intake 95A passed out of the college. From then on the college would run scaled-down eight-month foundation courses for REME and Royal Signals apprentices, joined in due course by trainees in the Royal Engineers and the Royal Logistics Corps. They would then go on to complete their apprenticeships at each corps' specialist establishments.

1997

January

Leather-bound minutes of meetings of the former Wokingham and District Water Company Ltd. were found abandoned in a skip by a Wokingham resident. After his death his widow took them to a specialist who suggested she take them to historian Cllr, Bob Wyatt. He agreed to restore them to their former condition.

January

Plans for the traditional town mayor-making ceremony were upset when Mayor elect Cllr. Fred Clark lost his seat on the town council in the local elections. Invitations had already been sent out for the event.

February

Wingmore Lodge in Rose Street was put up for sale by the owner, Celia Read, for offers of around £200,000. The lodge dates back to about 1750 and is a listed building.

1997 - 1997

Wingmore Lodge
© Jim Bell

May

John Redwood made a bid for the Conservative leadership. He also outlined his *Blueprint for Popular Conservatism* which was based upon the importance of listening to the people.

May

Wokingham Cricket Club's plans to move to Buckhurst were rejected by the inspector for the Department of the Environment.

May 9th

Since receiving a royal decree in 1219 granted by King Henry III Wokingham Market traded continuously in many forms over the 778 years from bartering for goods in medieval times to a cattle and pig market until the middle of 20th century. Its 778th birthday was celebrated by the Mayor Cllr. Tina Marinos and the market superintendent. They looked forward to promoting the market and making it a viable competitive business with Great British Market Week in August.

May 11th

A remembrance service was held in Wokingham Market Place in honour of George Knapp, a Wokingham wartime hero, fifty-one years after his death. He was killed two months after VJ (Victory in Japan) Day in 1945 and was buried in Kranji War Cemetery in Singapore.

1997 - 1997

June 5th

Brightly coloured aliens and astronauts touched down in Wokingham. But despite initial alarm, the visitors had landed in Wokingham to participate in the annual carnival with the theme *Space, the Final Frontier*. The floats were judged by Wokingham Mayor Cllr. Jack Earnshaw and Wokingham Round Table chairman Chris Liebert. The procession passed through the town centre where hundreds of onlookers lined the streets. Entries included those from Emmbrook After School Club, Wokingham Girls' Brigade, and Norreys Evangelical Church. The procession arrived at Cantley Field where there were many stalls and entertainments including a space ball which rapidly rotated thrill-seekers through 360 degrees. Music was provided by the St. Sebastian's marching band. The carnival procession was headed by carnival princess, Ria Poole of Ellis Road, Crowthorne. Funds raised went towards Daisy's Dream, a new charity to help Berkshire children to come to terms with bereavement, and Camp Mohawk, based in woods near Wargrave, where brain-damaged and autistic children could receive stimulating respite care.

June 5th

Instead of selling Wingmore Lodge, Celia Read decided instead to turn her drawing room into an exclusive small shop selling collectors' artisan porcelain dolls, teddy bears and traditional rocking horses made from mahogany, cherry, walnut and oak.

August

The 1996/97 air quality survey report revealed that air pollution in certain areas of Wokingham exceeded the national limit.

August

Elizabeth Hudson, granddaughter of a former Wokingham Alderman, contacted Wokingham Town Hall to offer to return an alderman's hat and gown dating back to 1900 together with original documents relating to the postponement of Edward VII's coronation in 1902, photographs of Wokingham Town Mayors and the order of service of the unveiling of a War memorial.

September

The people of Wokingham mourned the death of Princess Diana. The Council provided books of condolence. Leading community figures

1998 - 1998

including MPs Councillors, traders, charities and church congregations paid their last respects to the people's princess.

December

A hundred year old penny-farthing was restored to its former glory by K, C. Sports of Barkham Road and was in due course placed in the Courtyard Market in Wokingham Town Hall. This early type of bicycle was made in Wokingham in a blacksmith shop behind the Ship Inn in Peach Street. It was believed to have been be made for the father of bicycle dealer Jack Trill who with his brother Percy ran a family bicycle shop in Denmark Street. Mr. Trill donated the penny-farthing to the town as a historic memento.

December 11th

Historian Ken Goatley, affectionately known as Mr. Wokingham, was made Honorary Townsman. The ceremony took place at a civic ceremony in Wokingham Town Hall. Mr. Goatley gave a set of six silver spoons to the town in appreciation and paid tribute to his wife Edna.

Kenneth William Goatley
1927-2006

1998

January

People were baffled by the mysterious disappearance of Wokingham butchers Pettit and Brown. They suddenly closed the shop leaving a sign saying 'Gone for lunch' in the window. The shop's landlord stated that the company had gone into liquidation although this was not confirmed. The Official Receivers in Reading stated that Pettit and Brown Family Butcher was not on the list of those forced into liquidation or closed down by the courts.

1998 - 1998

February

Wokingham Councillors proposed to regenerate Wokingham Town Hall in a £700,000 millennium project to create something of a lasting value for the town. They wanted to give Wokingham Town Hall back to the people. About £100,000 was estimated to be required for maintenance work. Also included was modernisation of the kitchen and toilets; installation of a lift and ramps to provide disabled access to all floors; provision of adequate heating and lighting; a restaurant and cafe run by the town's young people; and improvement of the outdoor and indoor markets.

February

Howard Palmer Park off Howard Road was renamed Howard Palmer Gardens and underwent a number of improvements in time for summer. These included changing the entrance, moving some Victorian-style lampposts, adding benches, enlarging the flower borders and planting broad leaf trees. The Town Council also ran a competition among the junior schoolchildren in the town for the best picture showing where the nearest Town Council park was to their school, and what they most liked about it.(for example trees, flowers, play areas or animals).

April

Wokingham Football Club decided to sell its ground in Finchampstead Road to developers to clear mounting debts.

April 27th

The £30,000 MacMillan House extension at the cancer care day centre in the grounds of Wokingham Hospital in Barkham Road was officially opened by Wokingham Town Mayor, Cllr. Jack Earnshaw. These additions came eight years after Wokingham people raised £150,000 in a *Wokingham Times*-backed campaign to build the centre. Many of the fund-raisers were present. The extension which cost £30,000 included a reception area, a therapy room and disabled toilet.

May

Wokingham Town Mobility, a partnership between Wokingham Town Council and local businesses, was set up to provide scooters and manual wheelchairs to those with mobility problems. Volunteers were to meet the customer at a pre-arranged place where a period of training was given. The Town Council donated £2,000 towards publicity, insurance and maintenance and £3,000 towards administrative costs. Luff Group also made a building available in Broad Street Walk to store and charge the scooters.

May

Thousands attended Wokingham May Fayre in Denmark Street and the Market Place to enjoy May-Pole and Morris dancing and music from the Berkshire Youth Jazz Orchestra. A county fair was held at Elms Field, behind the old Tesco store, complete with bouncy castles, a rock climbing wall, and some farm animals, One of the highlights of the day was the crowning of the May Queen. There was also an art and flowers exhibition in Wokingham Town Hall.

July

West Forest Round Table, managers of the Summer Carnival due to take place on July 11, stated that there would not be a procession because of lack of enthusiasm. Only six organisations had expressed an interest in dressing a carnival float.

July

Wokingham Borough Council announced the temporary closure of the tennis courts and pitch and putt golf course on Elms Field to reduce expenditure, giving rise to fears of more development. The Council stated that it would reopen the facilities at the earliest opportunity.

September

Wokingham historian, Dennis Ayres died from a heart attack at the age of 77. He was a keen researcher and a leading light with Wokingham History Society and also contributed regularly to *The Wokingham Historian* and the Town Guide. Judith Hunter and Dennis compiled a book entitled *The Inns and Public Houses of Wokingham.*

October

Cllr Philip Harding, Town Mayor, accompanied by Stuart Brien, the regional manager, cut the tape and declared Marks and Spencer of Peach Street open. Minutes later the store was full of customers.

1999

Waitrose donated eight benches to be installed in the town.

1999 - 1999

January 30th

Emmbrook Post Office and Store, run by Sanjay Odedra and his wife Rekha, was officially reopened on Saturday by the Mayor Cllr. Phil Harding and his wife, Mavis. The store had been undergoing renovation since December.

February

Membership of Wokingham Town Mobility Scheme and the number of rides taken per week increased by 150% during the previous three months which led to requests for a paid co-ordinator. Wokingham District Council had a budget of £15,000 for boosting district-wide mobility but this was earmarked for capital use, which meant that it could only be spent on an administrator.

February 2nd

The barriers at Starlane crossing in Wokingham once again failed to rise. The crossing remained shut for more than 20 minutes while drivers sought alternative routes. According to Railtrack the delay might have been the result of "an unusual frequency of trains".

April 1st

The new police area covering the Reading Borough and Wokingham district areas including Woodley, Earley, Twyford and Wargrave came into operation. Previously Wokingham district had been split between the Reading and Bracknell Police areas, but it now came under one sector. The theme was problem-solving. There would now be one point of contact instead of two, with a view to improving communication between the service and authorities.

1st May

Wokingham Town Football Club, founded in 1875, played its last match on their home ground at Finchampstead Road. They were forced to sell the land because of spiralling debt.

1999 - 1999

June 4th

Karpinska Sculpture
© Jim Bell

A sculpture, depicting two children seesawing on an open book, was unveiled outside Wokingham library. The stainless steel base represents the book of *The Waterbabies,* by Charles Kingsley, former Rector of Eversley. The sculpture cost £10,000 and was made by Lydia Karpinska..

July

Wokingham Theatre secured planning permission to extend the north and west sides of its premises in Cantley Park. The project aimed to increase the 125-seat capacity auditorium by a further 18. The size of the foyer and bar was to be doubled and there would be enough space for a new box office and administration area. Backstage the £170,000 project would create improved lighting and sound facilities as well as more storage space.

July 8th

Workmen for Swan Hill Homes began to demolish Wokingham Town Football Club's grounds off the Finchampstead Road. The following season, commencing 14th August, the team was to play at Stag Meadow grounds in Windsor, sharing with Windsor and Eton Football Club."

August

Miss Isobel Elliston Clifton, former partner in Clifton Ingram, Solicitors, founded by her uncle, left £20,000 and most of her estate to the Wokingham Society. She had no connections with the Wokingham Society before her death in October 1998 so the bequest baffled and delighted Society members.

Isobel Elliston Clifton courtesy Wokingham Times

1999 - 1999

4th August

The market traders endorsed the Market Shoppers National Charter.

November

Thames Valley Air Ambulance took flight with activities controlled at the centre in Finchampstead Road.

November 3rd

The former tannery in Eyre Court, Finchampstead Road, was saved from demolition after developers and planners failed to agree. Millgate Homes had applied to demolish the tannery to redevelop the site as ten flats. But at a meeting of the development control sub-committee it was felt that the size of the new building would cause a loss of light for neighbouring residents. It was also decided that negotiations had gone on for too long so the application was refused.

2nd November

Sir William Radcliffe van Straubenzee, former M.P. for Wokingham from 1959 to 1987, died.

7th November

Gas cylinders exploded in a fire at Plough Farm, London Road. The fire was estimated as having been one of the most dangerous ever in the district.

29th November

Major John Lycett Wills, former 18th High Steward of Wokingham, died.

December

Plans were revealed to close Rectory Road police station. The station would be replaced with a town centre one-stop shop staffed by civilians, and open during the same hours as the existing station. The decision followed a nationwide review of the viability of police-owned buildings.

Addendum

The Wokingham Times went through a number of name changes during its life.

1903-1904 Wokingham & Bracknell Gazette and County Review
1904-1905 Wokingham, Bracknell & Crowthorne Gazette, etc.
1906-1914 East Wokingham, Bracknell and Crowthorne Gazette & East Berks Advertiser .
1914-1927 East Berkshire Gazette
1927-1930 The Wokingham Gazette and Berkshire County Advertiser
1930-1939 Wokingham Times and Weekly News
1939-1942 Wokingham, Bracknell & Ascot Times & Weekly News
1942-1948 Times & Weekly News
1948   East Berkshire Times & Weekly News
1948   Times & Weekly News
1948-1949 Wokingham, Bracknell & Ascot Times & Weekly News
1950-1956 Wokingham & Bracknell Times
1956-1957 Wokingham Times
1957-1959 Wokingham, Bracknell & Ascot Times
1959-1965 Wokingham & Bracknell, Woodley & Ascot Times
1965-2014 Wokingham Times

Sources

The Reading Mercury

Wokingham Times

Wokingham Parish Magazines

The Wokingham Historian by the Local History Group of the Wokingham Society

Wokingham A Pictorial History by John and Rosemary Lea

Wokingham the town of my life by Ken Goatley

Bygone Days In Wokingham *A nostalgic look back with Ken Goatley*

Kelly's Directories

The Sale Family History

Historical Notes on Wokingham by A. T. Heelas

Branch Lines Around Ascot by Vic Mitchell and Keith Smith

Gotelee's Compendium of Wokingham

Other Publications by Jim Bell

St. Paul's Wokingham Early 20th Century Parish Magazine Extracts
St. Paul's Parish Wokingham at War 1939-1946.
St. Paul's Parish Church, Wokingham
A Stroll through St. Paul's Parish Churchyard, Wokingham
19th Century St. Catherine's Bearwood Glimpses of Parish Life.
St. Catherine's Church Bearwood Parish Register Extracts.
A Short History of Bearwood and Sindlesham.
19th Century St. Nicholas Hurst Glimpses of Parish Life.
A Stroll Through St. James' Churchyard.
19th Century St. James Finchampstead,
First World War, St. James, Finchhampstead,
Memorials Inside All Saints Parish Church, Wokingham
Former Mayors of Wokingham, from 1885 to 1946
Former Mayors of Wokingham, from 1947 to 1979
Former Mayors of Wokingham, from 1980 to 2015
High Stewards of Wokingham
Former Town Clerks of Wokingham
A Short History of Five Wokingham Families
The Story of HMS Garth
Nine Days Holiday Tour in a Caravan
Miss Winifred Spooner, Aviatrix
Wokingham Remembers the Second World War
The Inimitable Cecil Culver
A Short history of Wokingham Fire Brigade
Wokingham and the Royal Jubilees
Memories of Wokingham Town Hall (1860 to 1946)
Memories of Wokingham Town Hall (1947 to 2005)
Miss Baker's School and other Wokingham Memories
A Chronology of Wokingham Home Front During WW1
A Short History of Wokingham